The Complete Guide to
Brewing Your Own Beer at Home

Everything
You Need
to Know
Explained
Simply

by Richard Helweg

The Complete Guide to Brewing Your Own Beer at Home: Everything You Need to Know Explained Simply

Library of Congress Cataloging-in-Publication Data

Helweg, Richard, 1956-
  The complete guide to brewing your own beer at home : everything you need to know explained simply / by Richard Helweg.
      p. cm.
  Includes bibliographical references and index.
  ISBN-13: 978-1-60138-601-4 (alk. paper)
  ISBN-10: 1-60138-601-X (alk. paper)
  1. Beer. 2. Brewing. 3. Brewing--Microbiology. I. Title.
  TP577.H4534 2011
  641.87'3--dc23
                            2011033260

Printed in the United States
PROJECT MANAGER: Crystal Edwards • cedwards@atlantic-pub.com
PROOFREADING: C&P Marse • bluemoon6749@bellsouth.net
BOOK PRODUCTION DESIGN: T.L. Price • design@tlpricefreelance.com
FRONT COVER DESIGN: Meg Buchner • megadesn@mchsi.com
BACK COVER DESIGN: Jackie Miller • millerjackiej@gmail.com

Printed on Recycled Paper

A few years back we lost our beloved pet dog Bear, who was not only our best and dearest friend but also the "Vice President of Sunshine" here at Atlantic Publishing. He did not receive a salary but worked tirelessly 24 hours a day to please his parents.

Bear was a rescue dog who turned around and showered myself, my wife, Sherri, his grandparents Jean, Bob, and Nancy, and every person and animal he met (well, maybe not rabbits) with friendship and love. He made a lot of people smile every day.

We wanted you to know a portion of the profits of this book will be donated in Bear's memory to local animal shelters, parks, conservation organizations, and other individuals and nonprofit organizations in need of assistance.

– *Douglas & Sherri Brown*

PS: We have since adopted two more rescue dogs: first Scout, and the following year, Ginger. They were both mixed golden retrievers who needed a home.

Want to help animals and the world? Here are a dozen easy suggestions you and your family can implement today:

- *Adopt and rescue a pet from a local shelter.*
- *Support local and no-kill animal shelters.*
- *Plant a tree to honor someone you love.*
- *Be a developer — put up some birdhouses.*
- *Buy live, potted Christmas trees and replant them.*
- *Make sure you spend time with your animals each day.*
- *Save natural resources by recycling and buying recycled products.*
- *Drink tap water, or filter your own water at home.*
- *Whenever possible, limit your use of or do not use pesticides.*
- *If you eat seafood, make sustainable choices.*
- *Support your local farmers market.*
- *Get outside. Visit a park, volunteer, walk your dog, or ride your bike.*

Five years ago, Atlantic Publishing signed the Green Press Initiative. These guidelines promote environmentally friendly practices, such as using recycled stock and vegetable-based inks, avoiding waste, choosing energy-efficient resources, and promoting a no-pulping policy. We now use 100-percent recycled stock on all our books. The results: in one year, switching to post-consumer recycled stock saved 24 mature trees, 5,000 gallons of water, the equivalent of the total energy used for one home in a year, and the equivalent of the greenhouse gases from one car driven for a year.

Author Dedication

Thanks to Karen, Aedan, and Rory for putting
up with all of my projects, no matter how much
space they take and how "stinky" they are.

Table of Contents

Chapter 4: The Necessary Equipment...................117

Chapter 5: Brewing for Beginners..141

Chapter 6: Extract Recipes............181

Chapter 7: Intermediate Brewing....203

Introduction

"**I**'ve always wanted to do that." This is a statement often expressed when the subject of home brewing beer comes up. This statement is usually followed by, "… but it seems so involved. I don't have the equipment or the space. I really don't even know where to start." This book is here to say, "You can do it." Brewing your own beer at home is fun, not as difficult as you may think, and economical, especially if you enjoy a variety of craft beers, or beers brewed using traditional brewing techniques and in small batches as compared to the popular beers brewed by the major industrial brewers.

According to the *New York Times*, a grassroots phenomenon has fueled the revival of craft beers in America over the past 30 years — so challenge yourself to create the best beers around for you and your friends. Whether you are into lagers or ales, the craft of home brewing beer is within your reach. Grab your beer stein and prepare to make this art form your next hobby.

You might have tried a great beer recently and want to know how to create something similar. With the various innovative methods outlined in this book, brewing like the pros is now easier than ever before. You will be able to start small and gradually learn to make more complex ales, lagers, and stouts over time, all while having a fun experience. This book will guide any prospective brewmaster through the process of making a unique brew — from inception to first pour. There are many advantages to making your own beer, starting with the low cost and the control you have over the maturity, strength, types, and volume of your creation. All of the rules and guidelines for home brewing have been laid out for you, along with the fascinating history of this popular beverage.

This book has been arranged to guide you from the basics about beer and brewing, to intermediate brewing processes, and then to more advanced brewing procedures. As the book guides you step-by-step through the process, you will first explore the history of beer followed by an overview of beer and the brewing process. The book will then expand on the information offered in the overview to guide you through brewing for beginners. Here you will learn more about the basic ingredients of brewing, detailed descriptions of basic brewing equipment, and basic brewing procedures. Once you have a handle on basic brewing, the book will explore intermediate and advanced brewing procedures. The book also includes a number of recipes for a variety of beers you may enjoy brewing at home.

Once you have gotten past the historical recipes offered in the first chapter, you will find a limited number of basic recipe types. For the sake of instruction, a number of recipe types are repeated as extract recipes (for beginners), partial mash recipes (for intermediate brewing), and all-grain recipes (for advanced brewing). That said, it is not meant to imply that advanced brewers do not do extract brewing. Many home brewers that are quite experienced and have been brewing for years only engage in extract brewing. You will see that the leap in the volume of ingredients needed to brew all-grain recipes may be a deciding factor in many a decision to stick to extract and/or partial mash brewing practices. By the end of your journey, you will have a tasty creation to call your own.

Beer experts from professional brewmasters to backyard microbrewers have been interviewed and asked how to best use these methods. Their tips have been provided to help get you through the complex process of beer brewing and production. Top homegrown recipes for beer are provided here that will allow you to create and enjoy your very own brews in the comfort of your home.

Enjoy your brewing adventure. If you are new to brewing, take this adventure step-by-step to ensure that you understand the ingredients, tools, and processes. Talk to people you might know who have taken this journey before you. You will be surprised how eager most brewers are to share their experiences, opinions, and knowledge. Finally, do not forget to share your beer with friends. You know that everyone is eager to taste the brew of your labor.

Have fun!

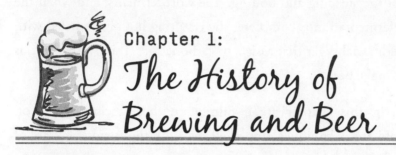

Chapter 1:
The History of
Brewing and Beer

The history of civilization is the history of beer. Beer was present when the pharaohs ruled ancient Egypt. Beer was certainly there on King Arthur's Round Table, aboard the Mayflower, and in the saloons of the old American West. Beer is one of the oldest and most revered of beverages, and beer brewing has taken place in homes and breweries for thousands of years.

Beer, by definition, is a beverage brewed, primarily, from malted barley, hops, yeast, and water. Brewing is the process of boiling and/or steeping ingredients in a liquid. So, brewing beer is the process of steeping and boiling malted barley and hops in water. The mixture, after steeping

Barley plants almost ready to harvest

and boiling, is called **wort** (pronounced "wert"). Yeast is added to the wort after the steeping and boiling. The wort ferments, and when the primary fermentation is complete, the resulting liquid is bottled with a little additional sugar that assists in carbonation. This, simply put, is how you make beer.

Included in this chapter are a number of beer recipes based on ingredients and techniques employed over the thousands of years of brewing history. Many home brewers, as well as some commercial brewers have attempted to duplicate these recipes. Doing so is a fun and educational foray into the science and practice of making this fermented grain beverage we call beer. Exploring these old recipes reveals the history of brewing and beer. The recipes will take you from the early days of a beverage brewed using little more than baked and soaked grain, to recipes that employ wild strains of homegrown yeast, through the more modern developments in the brewing processes developed in the 18th and 19th centuries.

If you choose to try some of these recipes, they offer a good education in the basics of brewing. As you begin to learn about beer and the brewing process, knowing how and why it developed the way it did will give you a good base to proceed from when you arrive at the later chapters concerning how to brew beer.

A Happy Accident

How beer was first discovered can only be speculation. Because the basic method of making beer is so simple, it is thought that beer was first made accidentally. Beer and bread are made from, essentially, the same ingredients, so it could be argued that they developed simultaneously and in similar manners.

It is believed that beer came about from a series of mistakes. These happy errors probably occurred in various locations about 6,000 years ago wherever grain was grown. The first brewers were most likely inhabitants of what is today Egypt, Iraq, Syria, or any of the eastern Mediterranean civilizations where grains such as barley were a staple. The first step in the discovery probably occurred when someone left a pile or basket of grain out in the rain. The rain soaked the grain, and after the grain dried, it was discovered to be somewhat sweeter than it was to begin with. This soaking had caused the grain to begin the germination process. The germination of the grain began the breakdown of the grain's stored starches into sugars. The result of this accident was malted grain, probably barley. Those ancient Mesopotamians discovered that this sweetened grain was wonderful for bread and a host of other dishes, but they still had not discovered beer. Another accident needed to happen for this discovery to be made.

The second accident that needed to happen was much the same as the first accident. That malted barley, whether it was bread or porridge, needed to be left out in the rain again, but this time for a longer period. Leaving this malted barley wet and out in the open air would invite some of the native wild yeast populations to feed on it. The yeast's feeding on this forgotten malt is what we call fermentation today. Someone who was very hungry must have found this fermented puddle because it would have presented itself as a bubbly, sour-smelling pool. However, when this sour liquid was consumed, it produced a feeling of relaxation and happiness.

This fermented liquid was the basis for beer, but note there was an ingredient missing from this early beer recipe of barley, wild yeast, and water. This early brew was hopless. Hops, the flowers used to flavor beer today, would not be used until the 11th century A.D. Also, note that the recipe below employs the services of a wild yeast starter. A wild yeast starter is grown from yeast that occurs naturally in air around you. This type of starter typically still is employed to brew a beer known as lambic. **Lambic** is exposed to wild yeast strains and ferments spontaneously. The first brews probably did not use this starter and, more than likely, relied upon a yeast strain that grew naturally on the grain used. This yeast was probably more like the baker's yeast used to make bread today. If you really want to go ancient, you might try making a brew with yeast cultured from a grain rather than the apple juice employed in the recipe below. The recipe here will yield a wild strain of yeast that feeds off the grain you provide. To do this:

Recipe for Wild Strain of Yeast

Ingredients

½ cup organic stone-ground whole wheat flour

½ cup + 2 Tbsps. unchlorinated spring water

Directions

1. Place flour and water in a sterilized bowl or wide-mouth jar. Stir the mixture well.

2. Cover the bowl or jar with a cheesecloth, and secure the cheesecloth with a rubber band or ring lid. Other than the cheesecloth, keep the top open.

3. Allow mixture to sit at room temperature for 12 hours. After 12 hours, add about 2 Tbsps. flour and 2 Tbsps. water to the mixture. Stir the mixture well.

4. Allow the mixture to sit at room temperature for about eight hours. After eight hours, stir the mixture again.

5. Allow mixture to sit for 24 hours at room temperature. After 24 hours, remove half of your mixture and replace it with an equal amount of flour mixed with water. To do this, mix about ¼ cup flour with ¼ cup water, and add to the remaining mixture.

6. Continue the process of removing half the mixture and adding fresh mixture every 24 hours. After a couple of days, you will start to notice that the mixture is beginning to bubble. This means that wild yeast is present. This may take as long as a week to ten days to occur.

Your mixture will be bubbly and have a sour smell. What you have made is a wild yeast starter. You can use this to brew or make sourdough bread.

The yeast should begin to ferment actively in about four to seven days, depending on temperature, humidity, and other environmental factors. You will note that the fermentation will cause the mixture to bubble actively. After the starter shows bubbles for an additional two to three days, it will be lively enough and contain enough active yeast to make it suitable for using. Taste the mixture, and you will recognize the sour taste of some sourdough breads you might have had. If the mixture begins to take on a rancid smell, you can attempt to "rescue" your starter. Do this by discarding 1 cup of the starter and mixing in 1 cup of fresh flour and 1 cup of water, then proceed with the normal feeding schedule.

Note: This yeast will yield a sour and nearly undrinkable brew. However, if you are really interested in tasting what the first "beer" might have tasted like, this is the way to go.

Using the apple juice in the recipe below will give you better chance at having something that might be a little more satisfying to drink. Though it probably will taste nothing like a draft from your neighborhood craft brewers.

The Brew of the Ancients

How to make the Brew of the Ancients:

Ingredients

Wild yeast starter (made with apple juice) — see directions below

Grain — Go to your local health food store and shop for a selection of grains that include hulled barley and a varietal selection of wheat, millet, and/or spelt. Be sure the grain you choose is organic. With organic grain, you can be sure that no additives that will affect your brewing. Get about 1 pound of barley and ½ pound each of wheat and another grain of your choice. The total weight of your grains should be about 2 pounds

Water — It is best to use water that is free of chlorine. Choose good bottled water or filtered water that is left to sit for several days to allow the chlorine to evaporate.

Directions

To make your wild yeast starter:

1. Pour 1 gallon of fresh, unpasteurized apple cider (organic is best), evenly distributed into quart-sized canning jars (four jars). Allow about 1 inch of room at the top of the jar. If you fill the jars to just below the top opening ring, that should suffice. This space will allow the bubbles room to form.

2. Cover each jar with a piece of cheesecloth, and secure the cheesecloth with a rubber band. Stir the juice two or three times a day.

3. After a couple of days, you will notice sediment collecting on the bottom of the jar. This sediment is yeast. You can use this yeast to brew the beer described below.

4. After three to five days of fermentation, use the yeast or replenish it by taking the yeast from the bottom of the jar and adding it to more cider. You can collect the yeast by scooping it up with a spoon or a spatula. If you do not do this, the cider will turn to vinegar. When you are done with the cider, discard it.

Note: If a green or black film appears on the surface of the cider during this process, throw it out, and start again. This film indicates that unwelcome bacteria has moved into your brew.

If an off-white to brown colored scum appears on top of the fermentation bubbles, skim it off as soon as possible. If it remains on the cider, the cider will turn to vinegar quickly.

The more you replenish the yeast; the more yeast will show up in the jar.

To brew your beer:

1. Start by malting the grains. To do this, begin as you would if you were going to grow sprouts at home. Mix the wheat and millet grains together, and place them, evenly divided, into two separate 1-quart mason jars. Put the barley in two jars. Cover the grains with cold water and swirl the grains around in the water. Cover the jars with a cloth or a screened sprouting lid (you can find these

plastic sprouting lids at health food stores or online at Wheatgrass Kits Organic Living Whole Foods Products (**www.wheatgrasskits. com**) and allow them to sit in a dark place at room temperature for 24 hours.

2.   After 24 hours, drain the grain. Rinse and drain the grain twice daily and keep in a cool, dark place between rinsings. Continue this process for a couple of days or until you notice the grain is starting to sprout. Be sure all of the grain has begun to sprout.

3.   As the grain sprouts, some significant chemical changes begin to take place. The grain, with the help of water and air, begins to produce enzymes that are vital to converting the stored and concentrated nutrients into everything the grain will need to carry on the life cycle. **Enzymes** are proteins produced in living cells that speed up or increase the rate of a chemical reaction such as the metabolic processes of an organism. Enzymes can increase the speed of a chemical reaction by up to a million times more than normal. By introducing that little grain to water, you have set a miraculous force into motion. The enzymes cause many changes as the grain sprouts: The stored carbohydrates are being transformed into simple sugars; complex proteins are being turned into amino acids; fatty acids, vitamins, and minerals all are increasing at incredible rates; and the sprout takes minerals and other elements from the water and binds them to amino acids. All of these complex activities are done to continue the plant's life cycle.

4.   Once you notice sprouting grain, or germination, rinse, and drain it one last time. Place the drained wheat mixture into the bowl of a food processor, and process it briefly so you have a mixture that is a combination of ground-up sprouts and some that are still whole.

Pour this mixture into a bowl and set aside. Place the sprouted barley onto the bowl of the food processor, and process it briefly so you have a mixture that is a combination of ground-up sprouts and some that are still whole. If you really want to go ancient on this recipe, you can use a mortar and pestle. Put the barley into a bowl and set aside. You now have two bowls of semi-ground grains. One bowl contains wheat and the other kind of grain you chose, and the other bowl has semi-ground barley.

5. Use your hands to form cakes the size of small saucers (about 6 to 8 inches in diameter) with the wheat mixture and half of the barley. Continue to keep the barley separate from the wheat. The cakes should be 1 to 2 inches thick.

6. Preheat oven to 125 degrees. Bake the cakes for one hour. Increase temperature to 150 degrees, and bake for another two hours. Increase temperature to 180 degrees, and bake for six to eight hours. By this time, the cakes will be a dark brown color, about the color of a dark stout.

7. Add 1 gallon of water to a large pot (a 3-gallon pot is good). Heat the pot to about 160 degrees. Put the barley you have set aside (the unbaked barley) into a cheesecloth bag or a steeping bag you use for brewing, and steep the barley for about 30 minutes at 160 degrees. If you do not use a thermometer, watch that the water does not come to a boil.

8. After 30 minutes, add the grain cakes to the pot. Steep these for 45 minutes.

9. Remove pot from heat and cool as quickly as possible by placing the pot in a sink full of cold water and ice. When the mix is cooled to about 100 degrees, transfer this liquid to a clean fermenting

bucket, being careful to leave most of the heavy sediment behind. Add enough water (at 70 degrees) to this mixture to bring your liquid to about 2 gallons. Thoroughly stir this mixture.

10. Add 2 teaspoons of your home-cultured wild yeast. You might have to experiment a couple of times to get this amount just right. Stir the mixture very well.

11. Cover the mixture and, to be safe, use an airlock. *See a description of airlocks in Chapter 4.* The airlock will allow the gas to escape the mixture and keep unsafe bacteria out.

12. Keep an eye on the airlock, and in a couple of days, you will notice activity. The airlock should bubble for a couple of days and then subside.

13. After three to five days, you can drink a somewhat flat beverage, you can bottle the beverage, or you probably will decide to do a little of both. Have a little taste of what you have brewed to see if you want to go any further. If you do, you can continue to bottle your brew.

    To bottle, mix about ½ to ¾ cup of honey with a cup of warm water. Pour this mixture into a large pot and add your fermented brew to it. As you transfer the brew, be careful not to transfer the sediment at the bottom of the fermenter. Stir the mixture well.

    Pour the mixture into clean bottles and cap them. You can use plastic soda bottles or glass beer bottles. With the plastic bottles, you can test for completion of conditioning by the hardness of the bottles. If you use glass, you just will have to crack one open in a couple of weeks to test it. The ancients did not bottle the beer. They just drank it!

Brew Note: Bottle conditioning is the process the brew goes through after it has been bottled. For the most part, the major activity that takes place at this stage is the carbonation of the brew.

There are a number of versions of this simple recipe. Most variations come in the way in which the grains are steeped. In these recipes, you would bottle the grains with water and honey and let the brew sit at room temperature for a couple of days, releasing the built-up gas every now and then. After several days, strain out the grains, rebottle with a little more honey, and allow the beer several days to condition before drinking.

The Most Ancient of Beverages

China is generally thought to be the birthplace of beer about 7000 BC. The Chinese brewed a drink called kui that was made with fermented grain. Kui also happens to be a mythological one-legged demon that invented music and dance.

The beer described in the previous recipe is loosely based on an ancient Sumarian recipe. Sumaria is the land that today is Iraq. "Beer" was not the word the Sumarians used; they had several different words for their brew such as *sikaru* and *dida*. In ancient Sumaria, the women were the brewers and made this wonderful beverage in their home kitchens. Thus, women were the first home brewers. The ancient recipe noted in the previous section was culled from a piece of ancient writing called

"Hymn to Ninkasi." Ninkasi was the goddess of brewing. The recipe is thought to be about 4,000 years old and is closely related to a product called bippar, which is twice-baked barley bread.

Around the same time in Sumaria, beer was written of in *The Epic of Gilgamesh*. *The Epic of Gilgamesh* is considered the oldest recorded story. It tells of the life and times of the King of Uruk.

> "Come now, Harlot, I am going to decree your fate,
> a fate that will never come to an end for eternity!
> I will curse you with a Great Curse,
> may my curses overwhelm you suddenly, in an instant!
> May you not be able to make a household,
> and not be able to love a child of your own!
> May you not dwell in the company of girls,
> may dregs of beer stain your beautiful lap,
> may a drunk soil your festal robe with vomit."

And

> "I butchered oxen for the meat,
> and day upon day I slaughtered sheep.
> I gave the workmen ale, beer, oil, and wine, as if it were
>   river water,
> so they could make a party like the New Year's Festival."

A major leap forward in brewing came in the 11th century when hops were introduced to beer in Europe. The introduction of hops served two purposes to those who brewed beer. First, hops gave beer a more satisfying flavor. Second, hops have certain antibacterial qualities, and beers brewed with hops will last longer than the ancient beers brewed without them. Hops' presence in beer does not kill bacteria, but they do prevent bacterial growth.

Brewers in medieval Europe also discovered that if they employed the different varieties of hops, they could make beers that differed in taste, depending on the variety of hop used in the brew. It was at this time, also, that brewers began to experiment with a variety of herbs and spices to give exciting new flavors to their brew.

Though it is not known exactly when hops came to be a part of the brewing process, Finland might well have the best claim to being the origin of the practice of adding hops to beer. The Finnish Saga of Kalevala, which was first written down in the 17th century, is from an ancient Finnish tale that describes the people of Finland and their beautiful country. The saga is made up of sections called runes. The 20th rune of the *Saga of Kalevala* is titled, "The Brewing of Beer." John Martin Crawford translated this excerpt from the *Saga of Kalevala* was into English in 1888.

Louhi, hostess of Pohyola,
Hastens to the hall and court-room,
In the centre speaks as follows:
"Whence indeed will come the liquor,
Who will brew me beer from barley,
Who will make the mead abundant,
For the people of the Northland,
Coming to my daughter's marriage,
To her drinking-feast and nuptials?
Cannot comprehend the malting,
Never have I learned the secret,
Nor the origin of brewing."
Spake an old man from his corner:
"Beer arises from the barley,
Comes from barley, hops, and water,
And the fire gives no assistance.
Hop-vine was the son of Remu,
Small the seed in earth was planted,
Cultivated in the loose soil,
Scattered like the evil serpents
On the brink of Kalew-waters,
On the Osmo-fields and borders.
There the young plant grew and flourished,
There arose the climbing hop-vine,
Clinging to the rocks and alders."

The text then proceeds to offer the recipe for a brew of historic proportions.

"Osmotar, the beer-preparer,
Brewer of the drink refreshing,
Takes the golden grains of barley,
Taking six of barley-kernels,
Taking seven tips of hop-fruit,
Filling seven cups with water,
On the fire she sets the caldron,
Boils the barley, hops, and water,
Lets them steep, and seethe, and bubble
Brewing thus the beer delicious,
In the hottest days of summer,
On the foggy promontory,
On the island forest-covered;
Poured it into birch-wood barrels,
Into hogsheads made of oak-wood."

Osmotar has a bit of a problem at this point of the saga in that the beer that was brewed from the ingredients she used did not sparkle. Try as she might, the beer was lifeless.

She enlists all manner and nature of beast and weather to bring life to her beer. Finally,

"Then the bee, the swift-winged birdling,
Flew away with lightning-swiftness
On his journey to the islands,
O'er the high waves of the ocean;
Journeyed one day, then a second,
Journeyed all the next day onward,
Till the third day evening brought him

To the islands in the ocean,
To the water-cliffs and grottoes;
Found the maiden sweetly sleeping,
In her silver-tinselled raiment,
Girdled with a belt of copper,
In a nameless meadow, sleeping,
In the honey-fields of magic;
By her side were honeyed grasses,
By her lips were fragrant flowers,
Silver stalks with golden petals;
Dipped its winglets in the honey,
Dipped its fingers in the juices
Of the sweetest of the flowers,
Brought the honey back to Kapo,
To the mystic maiden's fingers.

"Osmotar, the beer-preparer,
Placed the honey in the liquor;
Kapo mixed the beer and honey,
And the wedding-beer fermented;
Rose the live beer upward, upward,
From the bottom of the vessels,
Upward in the tubs of birch-wood,
Foaming higher, higher, higher,
Till it touched the oaken handles,
Overflowing all the caldrons;
To the ground it foamed and sparkled,
Sank away in sand and gravel."

HISTORIC RECIPE

Kalevala Ale

If you are feeling adventurous and would like to brew the ale of the ancient Finns, you might try this recipe gleaned from the ancient runes of Finland.

Ingredients (taken from the saga)

10 ½ lbs. malted grains

2 oz. hops

5 gal. water

1 cup honey

Fir cones and pine shoots to taste

Directions

1. Place water in a large pot, and heat to boil.

2. Add malted grains and hops, and allow them to steep for about half an hour.

3. Add fir cones to the pot, and boil for about 15 minutes.

4. Add pine shoots to the boil, and boil the entire mixture for 15 minutes.

5. Remove from heat, and skim off foam.

6. Add honey, and stir well.

7. Return to heat, and bring to a boil for 20 minutes.

8. Remove from heat, and cool as quickly as possible, preferably using an ice bath.

9. Cover with a large piece of cheesecloth, and allow a week to ferment. This brew, more than likely, was originally fermented as a large open vat. For this recipe, you can ferment in a container covered in cheesecloth and a loose lid.

Beer in the New World

Beer was brewed throughout most of Europe in this manner during the medieval and Renaissance eras. In the middle of the Renaissance, the brewing of beer was codified in Germany by the passage of a law called Reinheitsgebot, or the German Beer Purity Law. When you begin to consider how beer is brewed and what it is made from, you would do well to consider the German Beer Purity Law of 1516. Based upon Bavarian custom, the German Beer Purity Law states, "The only ingredients used  for the brewing of beer must be barley, hops, and water. Whosoever knowingly disregards or transgresses upon this ordinance shall be punished by the Court authorities confiscating such barrels of beer, without fail." If you have read carefully up to this point, you will note that the ingredient yeast is not noted in this law. The reason for this is that yeast had not yet been discovered. Yeast cells were first discovered by Dutch scientist Van Leeuwenhoek in 1719. The official law was updated in subsequent years to add yeast and wheat, but the law remained until 1987.

The German Beer Purity Law of 1516 was enacted for two reasons: health and economics. In 1516, the water available in the urban areas of Germany was not fit for human consumption. Brewing beer made the water more potable. The addition of hops and the fermentation into alcohol lent a certain amount of "sterilization" to the water. With so many people relying on their daily share of beer for basic hydration, the German Beer Purity Law ensured the beer was made with only safe and trusted ingredients.

According to a case study by Mari Anne Kocian on the subject published in 1997, "Would-be beer exporters to Germany and environmentalists rebelled for decades against the German beer purity law … Germans claimed that the law protected public health from harmful additives and public interest from misrepresentative advertising." The German law was lifted officially in 1987, but the tradition and history of the law continues to be felt in Germany to this day.

Beyond the borders of Germany, beer is often defined as an alcoholic beverage produced by the fermentation of any infusion or decoction of barley, malt, hops or any other similar products, or any combination thereof, in water containing more than 3 $^2/_{10}$s percent of alcohol by weight. (This is the legal definition of malted liquor in the state of Colorado.) The brewing process involves a number of stages that include malting young barley, extracting soluble malt with water, boiling the malted barley to create wort, and fermenting the wort with yeast. Finally, the brew is clarified, aged, and bottled or kegged. This definition gives the brewer a wide berth in creating a recipe.

With advances in the brewing process, some brewers began to substitute other grains that might have been more cost-effective in the initial stage. The use of these ingredients depended on the economics of the time and/or the environment of the particular brewery. But the German Beer Purity Law forbade any such substitutes. Because the law applied to any beer sold in Germany, not only beer made in Germany, the law ended up dictating the ingredients brewers all across Europe used, as no one wanted to be excluded from the profitable German market.

As to the economics of the German Beer Purity Law, the aristocrats, the lawmakers of the land, owned Germany's barley fields. By making it illegal to brew with anything but good pure German ingredients, the wealthy landowners basically were able to guarantee themselves a virtual monopoly on the grains used for brewing.

Germany was not the only country in Europe where beer was brewed, and each country on the continent seemed to develop its own particular style of beer. From the Bohemian countries in the east to the British Isles, beer was the beverage of choice in castles, alehouses, and farms.

At the time the German Beer Purity Law was enacted in the 16th century, the great powers of Europe were beginning to expand not only their expertise in the art of brewing, but also their reach across the Atlantic Ocean. By the middle and late part of the century, colonies were beginning to sprout up in a new America. With the colonies came beer. As settlers came to America, they brought their taste and style of brewing with them.

Adrian Block and Hans Christiansen were believed to have been established the first brewery in the New World on the southern tip of New Amsterdam in 1612. Today, this is the Battery Park section of Manhattan in New York City. Block and Christiansen were Dutch immigrants and considered the first commercial brewers in America. They probably brewed their beer using corn.

≻— HISTORIC RECIPE —≺

George Washington's Brew

In 1754, George Washington made note of a recipe for beer that was made for his family's consumption at Mount Vernon. This recipe has been preserved in the manuscript collections of the New York Public Library in a notebook kept by Washington. George Washington wrote the recipe.

"To Make Small Beer

Take a large Siffer [Sifter] full of Bran Hops to your Taste. Boil these three hours then strain out 30 Gall[ons] into a cooler, put in 3 Gall[ons] Molasses while the Beer is Scalding hot, or rather draw the Melasses into the cooler & St[r]ain the Beer on it while boiling Hot. Let this stand till it is little more than Blood warm then put in a quart of Yea[s]t if the Weather is very Cold cover it over with a Blank[et] & let it Work in the Cooler 24 hours then put it into the Cask — leave the bung open till it is almost don[e] Working — Bottle it that day Week it was Brewed."

In 1762, several years after George Washington noted his beer recipe, Michael Combrune published *The Theory and Practice of Brewing* in London. This is the first attempt to establish rules and principles for the art of brewing. This was the first book on this centuries-old practice.

"Whoever is attentive to the, practical part of brewing, will soon be convinced that heat, or fire, is the principal agent therein, as this element, used in a greater or less degree, or differently applied, is the occasion of the greatest part of the variety we perceive. It is but a few years since the thermometer has been found to be an instrument sufficiently accurate for any purposes where the measure of heat is required. And, as it is the only one Kith (we are acquainted with) which we are enabled to examine the processes of brewing, and to account for the difference in the effects, a theory of the art, founded on practice, must be of later date than the discovery of the instrument that guides, us to the principles."

To see the full text of Michael Combrune's fascinating *The Theory and Practice of Brewing*, go to **www.archive.org/details/ theoryandpractic00combiala**.

Early in the country's history, settlers were not able find the kind of ingredients they were used to brewing with. Alternatives to the grain and hop brew were experimented with, and brews made of the native pumpkin, or pompion as it was then called, were made out of necessity and desire for fermented beverages. There is an old American song of anonymous origin that goes:

> "Oh we can make liquor
> to sweeten our lips
> Of pumpkins, of parsnips,
> of walnut-tree chips."

HISTORIC RECIPE

Benjamin Franklin's Boyhood Brew

Much of early American brewing was still done in the farmhouse kitchens. Benjamin Franklin wrote in his *Poor Richard's Almanac* that as a child he enjoyed Poor Richard's Ale for breakfast. Although Franklin never gave a recipe for this "enjoy(able)" beverage, we can guess with some amount of certainty, due to available ingredients and other brews of the era, what its ingredients were and how it was made.

> "He that drinks his Cyder alone, let him catch his horse alone." BENJAMIN FRANKLIN, *POOR RICHARD'S ALMANAC*

If you are brave and would like to brew some of the "ale" that Franklin enjoyed as a child, this is how you might proceed:

Ingredients

2 Tbsps. stoneground cornmeal

1 slice of stale whole grain bread

2 cups warm water

¼ cup honey

1 Tbsp. of molasses or sorghum syrup

¼ tsp. ground spice (nutmeg, cinnamon, or a combination, perhaps)

¼ cup of yeast starter

Directions

First, prepare your yeast starter as described in the Brew of the Ancients several days in advance.

To make the beer:

1. Put 3 Tbsps. of cornmeal into a 1-quart glass jar

2. Add 2 cups warm water and ¼ cup honey to the cornmeal, stirring well.

3. Add 1 Tbsp. molasses to mix and stir well.

4. Add ¼ tsp. of ground spice(s) and ¼ cup of yeast starter to mixture.

5. Cover with an airlock and set in a warm place. Shake or stir this mixture once a day.

Note: An airlock can be anything that lets gas escape but keeps bugs and unwanted pests out. You can cover the jar with a folded piece of cheesecloth that is fastened around the jar top with a rubber band. You also can use a jar with a lid and loosen the lid a bit to have the same effect, or you can buy airlocks.

After brew has started to ferment, allow it to sit in a cool dark place undisturbed for three to seven days.

HISTORIC RECIPE

Pumpkin Ale

This description of a fermented pumpkin "ale" is from The American Philosophical Society, Philadelphia, and dated 1771:

"Recipe for Pompion Ale: Let the Pompion be beaten in a Trough and pressed as Apples. The expressed Juice is to be boiled in a Copper a considerable Time and carefully skimmed that there may be no Remains of the fibrous Part of the Pulp. After that Intention is

answered let the Liquor be hopped cooled fermented etc
… as Malt Beer."

By the year in which this recipe for "pompion ale" was written, America
was well colonized and farms that grew a wide variety of grains were
established. By this time, brewing was starting to move out of the
home, especially in the towns, and into local breweries and alehouses.

Bottling Beer and Creating the Industry

As America grew and successive waves of
immigrants came to her shores, they brought
their own beers and brewing styles with
them. The Dutch, English, Irish, German,
Scandinavian, and Slavic immigrants all
excelled in the craft of brewing, each with
their own particular take on beer. Breweries
and their attached alehouses, taverns, bars,
saloons, and inns became primary community
gathering places.

Early in their histories, these alehouse
breweries sold most of their beer on premises,
as the practice of bottling beer did not really
become common until after World War I. If
you wanted to have beer at home and you
did not brew your own, you would go to the
local brewery and have your growler filled.

This is a growler fit
with a stopper and an
airlock. Photo courtesy
of Rick Helweg

A **growler** is a container, whether a bucket or a bottle, that would be filled with beer at the local brewery. These containers were named "growlers" because of the sound they made while the CO_2 escaped the lid as they were transported from one place to the next.

Though bottled beer did not become a commodity until after World War I, it was not totally unknown before that time. It is believed that beer had been bottled as early as the mid-16th century. The first reference to the history of bottled beer and its supposed originator comes from Thomas Fuller's *The History of the Worthies of England Volume 2* written in the mid-17th century.

> "ALEXANDER NOWELL was born 1510, of a knightly family at Read in this county; and at 13 years of age being admitted into Brazen-nose College in Oxford, studied 13 years therein. Then he became schoolmaster of Westminster.

> "It happened in the first of queen Mary he was fishing upon the Thames, an exercise wherein he much delighted, insomuch that his picture kept in Brasen-nose College is drawn with his lines, hooks, and other tackling, lying in a round on one hand, and his angles of several sorts on the other. But, whilst Nowel was catching of fishes, Bonner was catching of Nowel; and, understanding who he was, designed him to the shambles, whither he had certainly been sent, had not Mr. Francis Bowyer, then merchant, afterwards sheriff of London, safely conveyed him beyond the seas.

"Without offence it may be remembered, that leaving a bottle of ale, when fishing, in the grass, he found it some days after, no bottle, but a gun, such the sound at the opening thereof: and this is believed (casualty is mother of more inventions than industry) the original of bottled ale in England."

The reason it took bottling beer nearly 300 years to become a common practice has to do with several circumstances. First, the quality of glass made several hundred years ago was such that most glass could not withstand the pressure of the carbonation that formed in the bottle. Second, quality glass was expensive. It is supposed that Nowell was fishing with his beer bottled in a clay bottle.

Old beer cask

One more reason that bottled beer did not catch on early was the perception that draft beer from casks was much better tasting. In 1691, Thomas Tryon wrote in his book *A New Art of Brewing Beere:*

"It is a great custom and general fashion nowadays to bottle ale; but the same was never invented by any true naturalist that understood the inside of things. For though ale be never so well wrought or fermented in the barrel, yet the bottling of it puts it on a new motion or fermentation, which wounds the pure spirits and ... body; therefore such ale out of bottles will drink more cold and brisk, but not so sweet and mild as the same ale out of a cask, that is of a proper age: besides the bottle tinges or gives it a cold hard quality, which is the nature of glass and stone, and being the quantity is so small, the cold Saturnine nature of the bottle has the greater power to tincture the liquor with its quality. Furthermore, all such bottle drinks are infected with a yeasty furious foaming matter which no barrel-ale is guilty of ... for which reason bottle-ale or beer is not so good or wholesome as that drawn out of the barrel or hogshead; and the chief thing that can be said for bottle-ale or beer is that it will keep longer than in barrels, which is caused by its being kept, as it were, in continued motion or fermentation."

From the westward growth and settlement of the United States to the early 20th century, America saw a growth in the number of regional breweries that produced a wide variety of beers based on the recipes of the immigrants that helped to settle the land. Breweries such as Yuengling® in Pottsville, Pennsylvania (which is currently the country's oldest continuously operated brewery); August Krug's brewery in Milwaukee, which became the Schlitz® Brewery; and George Schneider's Bavarian Brewery in St. Louis, Missouri, which was the beginning of the Anheuser-Busch® Brewery, are all examples of early breweries that became well-established brewers of regional beers.

A memorable year in the history of American brewing is 1840, in which Philadelphia brewer John Wagner introduced lager beer to the United States. Wagner brought his lager yeast with him from Bavaria with the hopes of establishing a brewery in the New World. John Wagner, however, never really became a large commercial brewer. He was, in fact, a home brewer. His foray into lager brewing marks the beginning of a monumental change in America's brewing and beer drinking habits.

Lager has become the preferred beer around the world, especially pale lagers and pilsners, because of their light and refreshing flavor characteristics. Although lagers are more difficult to produce because they require a cold fermentation, the rapid expansion of commercial breweries served the growing public thirst for lager. Over the next few years, lager was introduced in American cities such as Boston, Cincinnati, and Chicago.

If you would like to experiment with a mid-19th century beer recipe to get a taste of what beer must have tasted like in America before prohibition and before lager was the beer of choice in saloons across the land, you can try this ale recipe that dates back to 1882.

1892 Ale

Note: This recipe has been adapted to make it as easy as possible for the beginning brewer. Some of the methods described below can be adjusted for those more advanced brewers

Original Gravity (O.G.): 1.060

> **Brew Note:** Gravity is defined here as the density (thickness) of a liquid relative to the density of water. When you first mix your brew's ingredients together, the density is higher than it will be after the yeast has transformed the sugars into carbon dioxide and ethanol. The original gravity is a measure of the fermentable and unfermentable matter in the wort before fermentation. Final gravity is the measure of remaining sugars and solids in the brew after fermentation.

Ingredients for 2 gallons of ale:

6 ½ lbs. pale malt

1 ½ oz. hops

½ oz. priming sugar (table sugar or corn sugar)

Directions

1. Place the malt in a grain bag made for brewing. These bags are available at home-brew supply stores. *Several retailers are noted in the resource section at the back of this book.*

2. Place 1 ½ gallons of water in a large stainless steel pot and heat the water to 150 degrees F.

3. Mash grain for three hours in this water.

Brew Note: Mash — A fermentable starchy mixture from which alcohol, in this case beer, can be brewed or distilled. The verb, to mash, is to convert malt or grain into this mixture. To mash is to steep the grain (barley and other grains) in hot water, which activates the malt enzymes and converts the grain starches into fermentable sugars.

In step 2 of the directions above when you raised the temperature of the water to 170 degrees, you were performing a mashout. Raising the temperature halts the enzyme action.

4. Raise temperature to 170 degrees F for 30 minutes.

5. Sparge with hot water at 180 to 185 degrees F to O.G. or required volume.

Brew Note: Sparging is the act of spraying or sprinkling water over your mash to separate sugars that remain on the grain. There are many methods by which this can be done that we will cover in later chapters. For our purposes here, your sparge will be the no-sparge method. To do this, you will drain your grain bag as you remove it from your wort, though you should not squeeze the bag. Simply raise the bag up out of the wort, and allow it to drain into the pot. After the bag has drained, you will add enough hot water to bring your wort to the proper volume.

6. Bring wort to a boil and add hops.

7. Boil with hops for 90 minutes, and remove from heat. Cool as quickly as possible to about 70 degrees F by placing the pot in a bath of ice water.

8. Transfer to a primary fermenter, add ale yeast (try a White Labs Ale Yeast or an American Ale Yeast from Wyeast, a lab that makes yeast), and stir well to aerate.

Note: A fermenter is a vessel, a bucket or a large bottle, in which the brew is allowed to ferment for extended periods.

9. Seal the fermenter with an airlock in place. The brew will begin to ferment within 24 hours.

10. Keep an eye on the airlock after a couple of days. Once you notice it has completed bubbling (no bubbling for 48 hours), you may proceed to the next step. Generally speaking, you can keep a brew in a ferementer for up to three or four weeks before the yeast will start to affect the brew negatively. If brewers need to have their brew undergo a longer fermentation period, the brew is transferred to a secondary fermenter.

11. When you start to bottle, mix ½ ounce of priming sugar with 1 cup of water in a small saucepan, and bring it to a boil for two to three minutes. Pour the sugar water into a bottling bucket. A bottling bucket is a vessel that has a spigot attachment near the bottom to allow the brew to be drawn out of it. Brews are transferred from fermenters to bottling buckets just before bottling.

12. Siphon your fermented brew (wort) into your bottling bucket with the sugar water, avoiding the transfer of any of the sediment in your fermenter.

13. Gently stir this mixture to incorporate the sugar water into the wort.

14. Use a siphon to the fill the bottles to within 1 inch of the top of each bottle. Cap the bottles.

15. Mature in a cool, dark place for three months.

There will be much more on the mashing and sparging steps of the brewing process in later chapters.

Beer in the Time of Prohibition

George Schneider's St. Louis Bavarian Brewery was founded in St. Louis in 1852. Though Schneider had a difficult time making a go of it as a brewer, this year was a rather important year in the history of brewing in that it marks the birth of the brewery that would become what is today the largest brewery in the United States: Anheuser-Busch. Also, 1852 is the year that marked the beginning of a series of events that would change brewing and alcohol consumption in the country for a long time; 1852 was the year the movement that began prohibition took seed, as the states of Vermont, Massachusetts, and Rhode Island all enacted legislation outlawing the sale of alcoholic beverages. The laws were repealed in Massachusetts and Rhode Island, but this movement would not go away for another 80 years.

Through the later part of the 19th century and the early part of the 20th century, there was a growing concern among an increasing number of Americans that consuming alcohol was evil. Those who believed that alcohol should be made illegal for manufacture, sale, and consumption were known as **prohibitionists**. The arguments these prohibitionists made for banning all forms of alcohol were many and went beyond the strict moral argument that alcohol was evil and the places that made and sold alcohol also encouraged other such vices as gambling and prostitution. They also argued that alcohol brought with it health problems, economic concerns, social ills, and overburdened our legal system.

The issue of prohibition came to head in the United States in October 1919 when the National Prohibition Act, better known as the Volstead Act, was passed by both houses of Congress. The Volstead Act, named after Andrew Volstead, chairman of the House Judiciary Committee, became the 18th Amendment to the Constitution of the United States. The three purposes of this prohibition were:

- To prohibit intoxicating beverages
- To regulate the manufacture, production, use, and sale of high-proof spirits for other than beverage purposes
- To ensure an ample supply of alcohol and promote its use in scientific research and in the development of fuel, dye, and other lawful industries and practices, such as religious rituals

It also stated "no person shall manufacture, sell, barter, transport, import, export, deliver, or furnish any intoxicating liquor except as authorized by this act."

Those charged with enforcing this act discovered over the next 14 years that such a prohibition was impossible to enforce. Alcohol still was manufactured, sold, and consumed, though those that brewed beer had a considerably harder time of it through the Prohibition years and for a number of years after Prohibition was lifted.

Between the years 1919 and 1933, hard liquor such as gin was much easier to make and distribute than beer was. It was much easier for those that dealt in the illegal brewing and distilling of spirits, or **bootlegging** as it was called, to conceal smaller amounts of hard liquor than it was for the rather bulky brewing and distributing of beer. Beer brewing in the United States did not completely stop, but it dwindled significantly. During prohibition, many breweries turned to the manufacture of other things that their factories (breweries) were suited to. Some breweries remained breweries and made a product called near beer. Near beer is beer with an alcohol content below .05 percent. Some breweries went into the dairy business, sold milk, and made and sold ice cream.

Over the 14 years of the Volstead Act, it is said that America lost its taste for beer, or maybe it would be better said that they displaced their taste. Over this decade and a half, many of the breweries that had sprouted up around the country had closed. These breweries were not able to weather the storm that was the Volstead Act.

The 21st Amendment to the United States Constitution ended Prohibition in 1933, but it was not until the 1940s that brewing picked up steam again in the United States. It was unfortunate for the commercial brewers that remained in the United States that the Volstead Act was repealed in the midst of the Great Depression. This meant they had a difficult time financing their breweries and that their customers had little money to purchase their product. As the effects of the Great Depression subsided in the early 1940s and breweries once again were able to capitalize their operations, America once again had a growing thirst for beer.

Between World War II and the late 1970s, a handful of large brewers such as Anheuser-Busch, Coors®, and Miller Brewing dominated the American brewing market. These brews specialized in making refreshingly light lagers suitable to mass distribution. There was, however, an audience of beer drinkers that sought something different. The difference these drinkers sought was a return to the diverse varieties of pre-Prohibition America, as well as a more creative brewing universe.

Many of the beer drinkers that sought something beyond the mass-produced products of the large brewers turned to the practice of home brewing. These home brewers discovered that they could produce a large variety of unique brews. Many of these home brewers also discovered that many people just like them were interested in drinking these "craft" beers. This marked the resurgence of the small craft breweries, or microbreweries as they have come to be known, in the United States.

This growing interest in the art and craft of brewing has spawned not only a growing microbrew industry in the United States, but also the growth of the practice of home brewing.

CASE STUDY: TOM HORTON

I've been home brewing actively now for the better part of three years. I do it because I love it, and I love sharing it with friends and family. I caught the bug when my brother-in-law didn't have any place to store his home-brewing equipment. I offered to let him store some items in my house. Little did I know I would be using the equipment more than storing it.

I home brew as a hobby and as a way to experiment with my own ingredients. The only legality you have to worry about is distribution, and as long as you aren't selling your beer, I believe that you don't have anything to worry about. At least I haven't worried about it at all so far, and I haven't had any cops knocking at my door!

I enjoy the whole process from start to finish. Starting off with picking a beer — it's usually a collaboration with my brother-in-law — then shopping for supplies, and finally brewing the beer. The time spent with my brewing buddies while I'm doing it might just be the best part. Hanging out in my garage, drinking a few nice beers, huddled around a propane-powered turkey fryer — there's nothing better.

To me, the least sexy part of this process is the most important — making sure anything that comes into contact with the beer after the boil is sanitized. That includes siphons, bottles, caps, buckets, lids — everything. It's not the hardest, per se, but it is something that I need to remind myself continually. I haven't yet had a batch of beer go bad due to contamination, so I consider that my litmus test. One of the hardest things — for me — is to make sure I don't drink too much *during* the brewing process! I have to remember to take notes, and most important, I have to remember to measure the specific gravity (I forgot with a batch a while back).

I get a lot of recipes online, and I also have a book called *North American Clone Brews* by Scott R. Russell (**www.amazon.com/North-American-Clone-Brews-Homebrew/dp/1580172466**). The book is great in that it gives you recipes for different methods — you can use extract or all-grain, and either way you want to do it, the recipe is there for you. It's also fun to see how close you can come to your favorite beers or even brew clones of some beers you can't get in your area.

I don't really have a favorite type of beer to brew, but any beer that allows me to toss random items in to play with the flavor is great — which in my case is any beer! DIPA/IPAs (double India pale ale/India pale ales) are my favorite beers to drink. The hoppier, the better.

I would say that the most common mistake beginners make is in the reading of the recipes and getting an understanding of the timing of things before you start the boil. Also, it's good to know that it will take quite a long time for the wort to cool down before you pitch the yeast, so be prepared for this to take up most of a day.

Don't get discouraged if a beer doesn't come out exactly the way you like it. Use it as a learning experience. Also, clean, sanitize, rinse with hot water, dry, rinse, and repeat. I can't stress enough how important it is to keep things clean. Also — most important — have fun! This is a neat hobby that should be fun and exciting. It *will* test your patience, but it will be worth it.

Chapter 2:
An Overview of Brewing and Beer

s stated at the beginning of Chapter 1, beer, by definition, is a beverage brewed, primarily, from malted barley, hops, yeast, and water. Brewing is the process of boiling and/or steeping ingredients in a liquid. So, brewing beer is the process of steeping and boiling malted barley and hops in water. The mixture, after steeping and boiling, is called **wort**. Yeast is added to the wort after the steeping and boiling. The wort ferments and when the primary fermentation is complete, the resulting liquid is bottled with a little additional sugar that assists in carbonation. This, simply put, is how you make beer. The simplicity of the process bears repeating and remembering.

As you consider the activity of home brewing, you also may be asking yourself, "Is it legal for me to brew my own beer?" If you are at least 21 years old, the answer to that question is, "yes." You need to adhere to a few rules to brew your own beer, but it is perfectly legal.

The laws might vary slightly from state to state, but you probably are allowed to brew up to 100 gallons of beer per adult (person 21 years old or older) in your household. The only other rule that generally applies to brewing is that you cannot sell your beer. The beer you brew is for personal consumption. However, you can give your beer away. Friends love to be gifted a six-pack of great home brew.

If you have any questions regarding the legality of brewing in your area, you probably can get the answers from your friendly home-brew shop proprietor. If you do not have a local home-brew shop, you might want to check with local law enforcement.

Basic Ingredients

It is fair to say that what makes beer "beer" is the grain. The grain we are most interested in here is barley. Beer is brewed from malted barley. Specifically, beer is the product of fermented sugars extracted from malted barley. This sugar is known as **maltose**. **Malt** is a generic term for a variety of things associated with maltose and malted barley.

Malting barley is the process in which the grain is soaked and drained to bring about the germination of the grain. When the germination begins, enzymes are activated that begin to convert the starch reserves and proteins into sugars and amino acids. The brewer malts a grain to begin the release of these enzymes. Once the grain starts to sprout, it is dried to halt the release of the enzymes until the brewer is ready to use the grain.

When the brewer is ready to begin the actual brewing process, the malted barley is crushed and soaked in hot water to reactivate the release of the grain's enzymes, converting the grain's starch reserves into sugars. The resulting sugar is boiled with hops to produce the wort. **Hops** refer to the flower of the female hop vine, which is a member of the hemp family. Hops are one of the basic ingredients in beer.

The conical-shaped hop flower contains an essential oil with a very bitter flavor. The exact bitterness and aroma of the hop depend on the specific variety of hop. Hops contain alpha acid in the form of a resin that  gives them a bitter flavor. This bitterness works with the sweetness from the malt to create a more balanced beer. The alpha acid also acts as a preservative as it retards the growth of harmful bacteria while not affecting the fermentation process. Brewers balance the ratio of sweetness from the malt to bitterness from the hop in their brew by adjusting the type of hops used, when they are added to the wort, and how long they are boiled.

Hops are available to home brewers in two forms: whole and pellet. Whole hops are completely unprocessed. Pellets are pulverized hop flowers that are processed to resemble gerbil food. Whether you use the whole or pellet form of the hop will become a matter of personal preference. Generally speaking, pellets are available to the homebrewer in a greater variety. Most home-brew stores will have pellets in airtight packages available to the consumer. Fresh pellets will give you the exact results as fresh hops. *There will be further information on hops and their use in later chapters of this book.*

What has not yet been stated, though it may be a given, is that beer is an alcoholic beverage. There are nonalcoholic beers, but, for the most part, brewing beer is done to produce an alcoholic grain beverage. Alcohol is produced through the fermentation process. Brewing beer is the process of the yeast fermenting the wort to make beer.

Wort contains sugars to feed the yeast that make the alcohol in beer during fermentation. Yeast is added to the wort after the cooking process. Cooking the wort releases the sugars in the grains. Adding the yeast starts the fermentation process as the yeast feeds on the sugar. A home brewer can use two basic types of yeast, depending on the type of beer being brewed. To some extent, how these beers taste will be determined on the strain of top-fermenting yeast you use. During the fermentation process, the yeast feeds on the sugars, producing a layer of foam at the top of the wort. Top-fermenting yeast produces ale. Ale is a type of beer with higher alcohol content than that which is brewed with yeast that ferments at the bottom of the fermentation tank. Bottom-fermenting yeast is used to create lagers. **Lager** is a bottom-fermented beer that is fermented at cooler temperatures than the top-fermented ales described above. Lagers have a much crisper taste than the top fermented ales. Lagers are the most consumed and commercially available beers in the world and are the most difficult for novice home brewers to make because they demand a steady, cool fermentation and extended refrigeration necessary during the aging process. The distinct flavor of lagers is achieved by fermenting for longer periods.

The brewer adds wort to a large fermentation tank to begin the fermentation process. Occasionally, this step is achieved in the bottle. Yeast is added to the wort and stirred to ensure even distribution and aeration. The sugars in the wort feed the yeast,

Fermentation tanks in a large brewery

which breaks it down in a process known as **glycolysis**. Glycolysis gives the yeast energy, which allows it to multiply. The sugar is broken down into carbon dioxide and ethanol. Ethanol gives the beer its alcohol content, while carbon dioxide gives it its carbonation.

Brew Note: As you proceed in your learning, you will encounter the abbreviation ABV. ABV stands for alcohol by volume. Alcohol by volume tells you the percentage of the liquid that is alcohol. You will learn how to determine this using an instrument called a hydrometer in Chapter 4. While most beers have an ABV range of 4 to 6 percent, the ABV percentage of beer can range from less than 1 percent to 20 percent.

The last of the basic ingredients is water. The quality of water the home brewer uses is vital to the entire brewing process. Beer is, after all, 95 percent water. The home brewer should brew with water that is completely neutral in taste and has no odors. Use water that has no or limited chlorine, as chlorine will have a negative effect on the fermentation process. Excessive chlorine can be removed by boiling water for 45 minutes or by just letting the water sit in an open container for 24 hours. However you do it, the chlorine should be removed as any taste, aftertaste, or odor the water has will carry over to the final brewed beer.

If you want to be sure the water you are using in your home brew is chlorine free or suitable for brewing, use bottled water. Shop around for good, neutral-tasting spring water, and go with that.

Beyond the grains, hops, yeast, and water used to brew beer, you can use an endless number of additional ingredients to make your home-brewed beer distinctive. As your knowledge of the process increases and you begin to experiment with new recipes, you will encounter a whole list of herbs, spices, fruits, sweeteners, and other adjunct ingredients that you can employ in your brewing. *You will learn more about these ingredients and how to use some of them in later chapters of this book.*

Basic Equipment

Now that you have had a basic overview of the ingredients you will be using, you can become familiar with the basic equipment. To make a 5-gallon batch of beer (the amount that most home-brew ingredient kits will yield), you will only need a few basic pieces of equipment:

- A large pot that will hold and heat 3 to 5 gallons of liquid
- A fermenting vessel
- Transfer tubing

- A large spoon or spatula
- A thermometer
- A hydrometer
- A cloth steeping bag
- A priming container
- Bottles
- A bottle capper

As you learn more about the brewing process and more advanced procedures, you will learn about equipment such as wort chillers, mash tuns, brew kettles, and a whole host of equipment specifically designed for the advanced home brewer. *You will learn more about the specifics of the basic brewing equipment in Chapter 4 and the specifics of intermediate and advanced equipment in chapters 7 and 9 respectively.*

An Overview of Beer Types

As described earlier in this chapter, there are two basic types of beer: those made with top-fermenting yeast and those made with bottom-fermenting yeast. Beyond that, beer might be further classified in four main types: lagers, steam-style beers, ales, and wheat beers. Within each of these four types, there are scores of beer styles that range from American-style lagers to oatmeal stouts.

Lager

As described earlier in this chapter, lager is beer that has been cooled, fermented, and allowed to age under refrigeration. Also, lager is fermented with a bottom-fermenting yeast. Popular examples of lagers are Budweiser®, Miller Genuine Draft, and Heineken®. The following are the different types of lagers.

- **Amber lager** — Amber lagers are darker in color and slightly more flavorful than the popular American lager described below. This is a medium-bodied beer with a slight caramel character in taste and aroma.

- **American (or pale) lager** — This is the most common of beers as indicated by the examples noted above. American lager is closely related to pilsner (*see pilsner described below*), though it has a light to medium body and a crisp taste, and it is highly carbonated. American lagers often contain adjunct ingredients such as corn or rice. There is a notable absence of the taste or aroma of hops. Budweiser and Miller Brewing brew the most popular American lagers.

- **American "light" beer** — The U.S. Food and Drug Administration dictates what beer can be labeled "light" in the U.S. light lagers have 25 percent fewer calories than the standard American lager, are paler in color, are light in body, and are highly carbonated. Bud Light® and Miller Lite are popular examples of this beer style.

- Bock — Bock is quite the opposite of the light beer described above. Bock is a strong dark lager traditionally brewed in the winter for consumption in the spring. Bock is a malty beer with little or no hint of hop flavor or aroma.

- Doppelbock — This translates to "double bock." Doppelbock is darker and even more full-bodied than the bock beers with just a hint of hop to balance the malty sweetness.

- Dortmunder — This lager originated in Dortmund, Germany, and is a golden-colored lager that is more full-bodied than the pilsner, though it is considered a pilsner-style lager.

- Dunkel — "Dunkel" is the German word for "dark." Dunkel beers are dark lagers. Dunkels are the original lagers and have been brewed for a longer time than the lighter lagers such as pilsner and Dortmunder. Though dark, Dunkels are not as strong as the Doppelbock.

- Munich Helles — As the name implies, Helles is a lager that originated in Munich, Germany. Munich Helles is a medium-bodied lager that ranges in pale to golden in color. The beer has a good balance of malt and hops.

- Pilsner — This lager originated in Bohemia and central Europe. Pilsner is a medium to full-bodied lager with a medium showing of hops and a good amount of carbonation. A wide range of pilsners are sold commercially such as Amstel®, Grolsch®, and Heineken. It should be noted that pilsners are best when they are fresh. A good sign of a fresh pilsner is a dense head when poured or drawn.

- **Vienna lager** — This medium-bodied amber- to red-colored lager originated in Vienna in the 19th century. The lager has a soft malty flavor. This lager is most popularly brewed in Mexico as Dos Equis®.

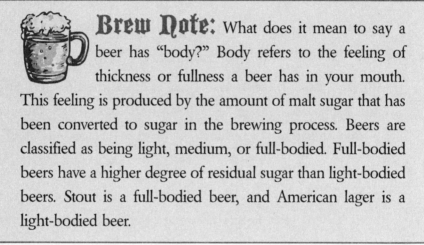

Brew Note: What does it mean to say a beer has "body?" Body refers to the feeling of thickness or fullness a beer has in your mouth. This feeling is produced by the amount of malt sugar that has been converted to sugar in the brewing process. Beers are classified as being light, medium, or full-bodied. Full-bodied beers have a higher degree of residual sugar than light-bodied beers. Stout is a full-bodied beer, and American lager is a light-bodied beer.

California Common/Steam beer

California common, or steam beer, also might be included in the lager beer family of beers, but it is set apart for several reasons. First, steam beer is the only truly original American beer, as it is a style of beer developed in the American West. Second, although this beer is brewed using lager yeast, the manner in which the yeast is fermented has been adapted to meet the environment in which it was originally brewed. Steam beer originated in California in the 19th century. The time and place of this beer's origin indicate that refrigeration was not widely available. This being the case, brewers were forced to be creative in the way they quickly cooled their beer (the reason for which you will understand when you brew your first batch of beer). To help them cool their brew more quickly, brewers chose to employ shallow fermenters. To describe the fermenting process and the type of beer it produces more simply might be to say that Steam beer is a lager that is fermented at ale temperatures.

The reason that this beer is called "steam" beer is anecdotal. Several different stories exist as to the naming of steam beer. The Anchor Brewery copyrighted the name "Anchor Steam® Beer" in 1981, as they originated the brewing process. One story says that to cool the beer, the brewery pumped it to shallow tanks on the roof of their brewery to cool. When the beer got to the rooftop, it would give off steam that always seemed to hover over the brewery, thus, Anchor Steam Beer. Today, any other beer made in this manner must be called California common beer.

Steam beers are medium-bodied beers that are slightly malty in character and have a good hop presence. The beers are, generally, light amber in color.

Ale

Ale is a general name for beers brewed with top-fermenting yeast. As a beginning brewer, you will probably begin your adventure by brewing one of the styles of ales listed here. The list included below is by no means all-inclusive, as there are scores of styles of ale brewed world-over. Included here is a list of the most popular and widely brewed ales.

- **American ale** — A wide berth of interpretation should be given to this category of ale. There are those who might say the U.S. does not have an original ale in the way that steam beer is native to the lager family. In 2008, Budweiser introduced a product called Budweiser American Ale meant to appeal to the beer drinkers looking for a flavor slightly more robust than its famous lager. On the other hand, craft brewers might indicate that ales brewed strictly with American hops are American ales. This is ale in search of a personality. Perhaps the new brewer reading this book will define truly original American ale?

- **Barley wine** — The name misleads, as barley wine is a beer in the ale family. The wine moniker has been attached to this ale because of its exceedingly high ABV. Barley wines can have up to 15 percent alcohol content. Barley wine also compares to traditional wine in that it is often aged for long periods. Barley wine can come in a variety of characters from sweet to highly hoppy.

- **Belgian ale** — A book could be written on this category of ales alone. Charlie Papazian in his book *The Complete Joy of Home Brewing*, refers to Belgium as "the Disneyland of the beer world." This statement is aptly put. Belgian ale is a catchall term for any ale brewed in Belgium. The ales in question range from Belgian white ale to lambic, and Belgian strong ale.

  - White ale is a somewhat cloudy wheat ale that gets much of its flavor from the additions of coriander and orange peel. To be defined as a white beer (or witbier to the Belgians), there needs to be at least 25 percent wheat malts used.

  - Lambic is a beer brewed in a most unconventional manner in that it does not employ brewers yeast, but employs spontaneous fermentation via wild yeast strains present in the air of the brewery. The resulting beverage is sour and quite unique compared to other beers. Many brewers employ fruits such as raspberries or cranberries in their lambic.

  - Belgian strong ale is a sub-category in the Belgian ale family in that these ales can be light or dark. The operative word in this category is "strong." "Strong" here mean that the ale has a higher than normal ABV that may range from 7 to 12 percent.

- **Brown ale** — This classic British ale is a great old-style beer. Brown ale, sometimes called nut-brown ale, has a medium body, is mildly sweet, and has a low hop profile.

- **Cream ale** — Though this beer is called ale, it is not uncommon for cream ale to be made with lager yeast. Often, the brew is fermented with top-fermenting ale yeast and finished with lager yeast. As such, this is a hybrid brew. Cream ales can have the mixed characteristics of a crisp lager, as well as the hopped nature of a good hoppy ale.

- **Irish red ale** — This is well-balanced ale with a slightly sweet taste and lightly hopped. As the name implies, Irish red ale has a slightly red hue from the small amount of roasted barley used in its brewing.

  - Flanders red ale gets its name from the red malt used in its brewing. This ale is a member of the sour ale family, and much of its flavor comes from the fact that it is fermented using a lactobacillus culture. The sour taste derives from the production of lactic acid.

- **Oatmeal stout** — Dark, hearty ale, oatmeal stout is a sweet brew that is made with 5 to 10 percent oatmeal in the brewing process. The presence of oatmeal gives the beer a smooth and creamy character.

- **Old ale** — This title is given to strong dark ales that are, for the most part, brewed in England. Old ale will have an ABV above 6 percent.

- **Pale ale** — This type of ale is another of those that has an extensive family tree. Pale ale is the name given to beers that are brewed with top-fermenting yeast and pale malt. Some of the beers that belong to this family are amber ale, English bitter, Scotch ale, and India pale ale.

  - Amber ale is something of a catchall term for ales brewed with malts that give them their amber hues. These ales can range from having only a slight hop characters to being extremely hoppy.

  - Bitter is ale that takes its name from the "bitter" sensation hops provide. These beers can range in hue from copper to gold and are light on the ABV scale.

  - India pale ale is a highly hopped light ale with a bold hop taste. Also referred to as IPA, this beer is said to have gotten its name as it was first brewed in England and shipped to India by the East India Company. Double IPAs are made with a higher concentration of hops, making them extremely "hoppy" brews.

  - Scotch ale is strong dark ale that has a prominent malt presence. It is not uncommon for Scotch ale to have an alcohol volume of 8 or 9 percent.

- **Porter** — This dark brown to black ale is, quite possibly, one of the most complex beers. Porter is a strong dark beer made of a blend of pale, black, chocolate, and other types of malt. Porter gets its name, it is said, from the British transportation workers that favored the brew in the 1700s.

- **Stout** — Aptly named, stout refers to the strong character and ABV of this brew. Stout is a sweet, dark, malty brew that is creamy and forms a great soft head when poured or drawn from the keg.

Wheat beer

Generally, beer brewed with 25 to 100 percent wheat malt is considered a wheat beer, with the balance of the employed malt being barley. Under the heading of wheat beers, there are a great many styles, a few of which are described here. The reader may know this beer as weizen, weissbier, or the previously described Belgian wit. The American equivalent is "wheat beer," though there are significant differences within this family tree.

- **Hefeweizen** — The name of this beer translates from the German "hefe weizen" to "yeast wheat." This beer is identified not only by the presence of wheat, but also by the particular type of top-fermenting yeast. The combination of the wheat and "hefe" give the beer a slightly fruity taste. This beer is very lightly hopped.

- **Berliner Weisse** — This is a very sour beer with very high-malted wheat content (60 to 75 percent). This beer is fermented not only with the top fermenting yeast, but also with a lactobacillus culture. Lactobacillus is a bacterium that helps to convert lactose and other sugars into lactic acid. This is a culture commonly found in dairy products such as yogurt and buttermilk. The combination of ingredients in this beer gives it a citrus-like sour taste.

- **Dunkel Weizen** — This is a traditional dark wheat beer. The name translates to "dark wheat." The darkness of the brew is the result of the dark roasted malted barley that is combined with the wheat. The beer is a medium-bodied brew with an almost bread-like flavor.

- **American wheat** — American wheat is a more subtly flavored version of its European wheat beer cousin. The beer still has a slight yeast tartness to it, but not at the level of the hefewizen and certainly not at the Berliner Weisse level.

The overview of brewing and beer presented in this chapter only skims the surface of the ingredients, equipment, processes, and beer styles in the great world of beer and brewing. The following chapters of this book will explore the development of beer and brewing and lead you step-by-step though the particulars of the brewing your own beer. With each step, you will learn, more specifically, how the ingredients and equipment noted above work to create this world of beers.

CASE STUDY: ERIC HOLDEN

www.drunkreddragon.com/
recipes.html

I am currently the brewmaster for the Temecula Valley Homebrewers Association. I also do my best to teach the love of good beer to all others, both in craft brewing and home brewing. I brew about 190 gallons of beer each year.

I had been wanting to home brew for quite a while but never really made that first step. One of my friends was getting out of home brewing and was giving away his gear. I took it off his hands and made my first trip to a home-brew store. I grabbed all my ingredients and made my first batch that day. I started small with a 2-gallon kettle. Since then, I have gone to a 15-gallon brewing system of my own design.

I have brewed with commercial breweries before as prizes for winning of home-brew competitions and found that it is almost exactly the same process just on a larger scale. Home brewers do have to follow some guidelines. In California, it is legal to home brew up to 100 gallons per year per adult in the household with a maximum of 200 gallons per year per household. I follow this law. We cannot sell our beer in any way, shape, or form.

I enjoy home brewing for the same reason that I like to cook — to see the pleasure of others enjoying something I have made. Sure, I like good beer, but to be able to give it to someone else and have them enjoy it, that is the real reason for my brewing. You get to use your imagination and come up with new and exciting recipes or brewing techniques and then share those with others. Also, I enjoy good beer, and the fruit of your own labor always tastes the sweetest.

The hardest thing about home brewing is either finding the time for it or wanting to achieve perfection. The brewing process takes about eight hours, and you can't really stop one day and start another — you only get about 45-minute breaks at any point in time. The other problem is wanting to create that perfect beer that has no flaws. You can always detect even the littlest problems in your beer. Being a musician, you notice when you make a slight error, and while the audience (or drinkers in this case) may never notice or detect it and in the end, they love it, you always know. I determine my success by the amount of medals on my wall. Sure, this might sound egotistical, and I am to some extent, but I love competing in home-brewing competitions and winning medals. It is validation that I have produced a quality product.

My favorite beer recipe is Russian imperial stout. I have brewed perhaps a dozen different recipes, but this one has been my favorite. It took 2nd place at the Stone AHA home-brew competition last year. (You can find that recipe at **www.drunkreddragon.com/ BeerRecipes/64.html**.) My favorite beers to brew are sours such as a lambic or Flanders red. The reason for this is that these are beers that take years to make and develop the characteristics of a good example of the style. You have so much riding on the beer, and you don't know if it will be good until at least a year from when you made it.

Russian imperial stouts are my favorite beers to drink. I love thick, malty, roasty, and black stouts. Individually, Alesmith Speedway Stout is my No. 1 favorite beer for drinking.

The most common mistake that new home brewers make is worrying. So many home brewers worry about this or that, about if their beer is ruined, but to quote the godfather of home brewing, Charlie Papazian, "Relax. Don't worry. Have a home brew." Making beer is easy; you can get way too in-depth with temperatures, pH levels, enzymes, and water alkalinity, but in the end, you are just making beer, so relax! If you can make a stew, you can make a beer.

Have fun! Experiment and try new ingredients. Join your local home-brew club, talk with others about their mistakes, and get advice from elder brewers. Home brewing is a great hobby, and I have never met a brewer of beer that is without friends. Just make beer you enjoy. As was once said, "Beer is proof that God loves us and wants us to be happy."

Chapter 3:

The Necessary
Ingredients

ow that you have had an overview of the craft of making
your own home brew and are familiar with the history of
the practice, you can start to really dive into beginning to
brew your own beer at home. This chapter will explain the ingredients
you will need to brew your first batch of beer. Because you may choose
to take several different paths as you begin, this chapter will describe
basic ingredients that may have been outlined in the German Beer
Purity Law you read about in the first chapter. This chapter also will
explain a prepackaged home-brewing kit and describe the ingredients
you would be likely to find in one of these products.

You will recall that the German Beer Purity Law that was discussed in
Chapter 1 stated, "The only ingredients used for the brewing of beer
must be barley, hops, and water." You will also recall that the official
law was updated in subsequent years to add yeast and wheat, but the
law remained strict until 1987.

To bring this list of basic ingredients up to date and to make it more
practical for you, the 21st century American home brewer, we will add
several more ingredients to this list:

- Malt extract
- Sugars
- Spices and flavorings

Barley

Beer begins with barley. Malted barley is the base for most beer. Wheat, rice, and corn also commonly are used for brewing, but malted barley is the most common starting point in the brewing process. Barley is a cereal grain that, according to the U.S. Grains Council, "has been adapted to the widest variety of climates, from sub-Arctic to sub-tropical. Barley is grown on a wide scale in Russia, Australia, Germany, Turkey, and North America. Leading exporters are the European Union, Australia, and Canada."

As you start to read various recipes for brewing, you will note that many recipes call for six-row or two-row barley. These descriptions refer to the way barley is classified. Six-row and two-row describe the physical arrangement of kernels on the barley plant. The difference in these two types of barley might be negligible to the small home brewer, but two-row barley has a higher starch content than six-row barley and will yield a greater amount of malt extract. Also, some brewers state that the larger kernels of the two-row barley yield a better tasting beer. The case to be made for six-row barley is that it is more adaptable to a wider variety of climates and is somewhat easier to grow. Advances in barley breeding practices over the past several decades have nearly erased any taste differences between two-row and six-row barley varieties.

Barley used to brew beer must be malted. The malting process involves steeping the barley grains in water until they begin to sprout. *This process was described in Chapter 1.* The sprouted grains, known as green malt, are then allowed to dry and then are roasted.

Brewers consider a number of things when deciding which type(s) of barley malts to use in the beer they are brewing. When considering what type of malt to use in their mash, the brewer will take into account the yield of sugar from the malt. This is referred to as **extract**. The brewer will consider the **diastatic power** of a particular malt, which refers to the enzymes in the malt that convert starch to sugar during mashing. Brewers also consider color when they choose their grain malt. The color of a grain malt is, generally, attributed to the scale of curing in the roasting process. This curing affects both the color and taste of the final brewed product.

Malts, basically, are divided into two categories, base malts and specialty malts. As a beginning brewer, you will, most likely, use malt extract for your base malt. Malt extracts are base malts that already have been mashed. Base malts are the primary source of the diastatic power in any recipe. Diastatic power is the enzymatic power of the malt. This defines the malt's power to break down starches into even fermentable sugars during the mashing process. The word "diastatic" is used in reference to "diastase" enzymes.

Base malts are the primary malt in any recipe. There are three important things to know about these malts:

1) **Must be mashed:** Base malts must be mashed to convert their starch into fermentable sugars and dextrins. Mashing continues the enzymatic breakdown that was begun during the malting process and breaks down the long-chain sugars to enable the yeast to consume them during fermentation.

2) **Diastatic power:** Base malts are higher in enzymes than specialty malts. The roasting process the specialty malts go through destroys much of their diastatic power.

3) **Fully modified:** Most base malt varieties have been modified fully to allow them sufficient enzymatic viability. This means they are able to mash both themselves and 20 to 40 percent of adjuncts or non-enzymatic grains.

There is a minor exception to the last point regarding modification: Not all base malts will be modified fully. There is a category of base malts that are labeled as "under-modified."

Modification is the complex stage of the grain development as the individual grain goes from seed to growing plant. Modification describes the degree to which the protein and starches of the grain have been broken down. A grain is considered fully modified when the embryonic barley plant, or acrospire, is about three-fourths the length of the grain. The acrospire is the scientific name for the first shoot that develops from a germinating seed. An under-modified malt is a grain in which the acrospire has appeared, but it is only about half the length of the grain. This means that a more complex process needs to be undertaken by the brewer to use these malts. Examples of under-modified malts are:

Budvar Under-Modified Pale Moravia — This malt needs to be mashed using multiple temperatures. The name "Bud" may be familiar as it is the malt used by the "original Budweiser" brewery, Budweiser Budvar.

 Brew Note: The brew named Budweiser Budvar is not the Budweiser Beer known in the United States but is the beer that has been brewed since 1785 in České Budějovice (Budweis), Bohemia. This particular beer is sold in the United States under the trade name Czechvar because Anheuser-Busch owns the United States copyright to the name Budweiser.

Spitz Malz — Meussdoerffer Spitz is an under-modified malt that can be employed in conjunction with a pilsner or any other highly modified malt. Used in this manner, this malt is known to enhance the beer's color and improve its head retention.

There will be more about under-modified malt in Chapter 9 when all-grain brewing is described. These malts need to be mashed in a process known as step mashing.

As you proceed through the next few chapters and get into the various recipes in this book, you will note that there is a difference in the types and purposes of malts and their uses in extract recipes compared to all-grain recipes. Extract recipes will derive most, if not all, of their fermentable power from the malt extracts added to them. Grains are used in most of these recipes, but they are known as "specialty grains." Specialty grains are used to add flavor, color, fullness, mouth-feel, and character to your beer. Roasting the specialty grains gives them their color. The more the grain is roasted, the more color it will have. Unfermentable sugars in the specialty grains make beer sweeter.

The world of grain malts is a vast one and includes many different malt styles. You will learn about a number of different malt styles as you work your way through this book, but for now, we will describe the most common malts you will encounter in your beginning brewing adventure.

Common malts

- **Pale malted barley** is roasted, or kilned, only enough to dry it. Barley malted in this fashion produces the most sugar compounds during the mash because it has a high degree of starch. Pale malted barley is the primary ingredient in most beers, both light and dark, due to its large degree of fermentable sugar.

- **Amber malt** is malt that has kilned slightly longer and at slightly higher temperatures than pale malt, which gives it a slightly darker color. Amber malt is commonly used in making porter, though it is not widely available to brewers today. Those who choose to use amber malt can produce their own product by toasting pale malt in their home oven.

- **Crystal malt** is processed in a manner quite different from the process that produces pale malts in that it is wetted and roasted in a rotating drum before kilning. This process converts the starch in the barley into fermentable sugars before the kilning. Thus, when the product is kilned, the sugars crystallize.

Photo courtesy of
www.KirksBrew.com

   Using crystal malts will increase the final sweetness of the beer.

- **Chocolate malt** is not chocolate at all but dark roasted barley malt. "Chocolate" refers to the color of the malt as it is roasted at high temperatures. Ironically, chocolate malts add flavors closer to vanilla or caramel than to chocolate to the brew. These malts are used for beers such as porters and stouts.

- **Black malt,** as the name implies, is malt that is even darker than chocolate malt. This malt is kilned at higher temperatures than chocolate malt and has the color of a dark espresso. These malts are used in the darkest of beers such as porter and stout. You might also see this malt referred to as black patent malt, as the process for making this malt was patented by a fellow named Daniel Wheeler in England in 1817.

- **Malted wheat** is the primary grain in wheat beers. Beers brewed with more than 25 percent malted wheat are considered wheat beers. One of the issues the brewer encounters with malted wheat is that there are few enzymes in wheat, so it is often desirable, though not necessary, to mix the wheat with barley. Remember, it is enzymes that work to convert starch to sugar. Wheat has a much higher protein content than barley. This high protein content can sometimes result in chill haze. **Chill haze** is caused by suspended particles in the beer that scatter light as it passes through the beer. The insolubility of the protein content of the wheat is brought on as the beer wort cools. Chill haze does not affect the taste of the beer but does give it an opaque quality.

• **Malt extract** is highly concentrated wort and comes as either a liquid or a dried extract. Extracts are produced in the same manner that wort is as crushed malted barley is mixed with water and mashed. The mashing converts the starch compounds into fermentable sugars. To convert this wort into malt extract, water is evaporated from the wort, leaving thick syrup that is the extract.

For the beginning or intermediate home brewer, malt extract is the way to go as it cuts the time it takes to produce a batch of wort for fermentation into beer. Using malt extract is a convenient way to brew beer at home.

Malt extract is most commonly available as a liquid in the thick syrup form, but it is also available in a dried powder form. The powder is more expensive than the syrup because it involves a greater amount of energy to produce. Brewer's preference for dry and/or liquid extract will vary from brewer to brewer and might even depend on the specific type of beer being brewed.

As you explore the world of malt extracts, you will discover that you have a choice of hopped or unhopped extracts. Hopped extracts are malt extracts that have hops already added to them, thus eliminating yet another step in the home-brew process. Choosing hopped extracts might be good for the beginner brewer who is exploring the craft for the first time, but as you learn and progress in your knowledge of the craft, you will probably want to move away from hopped extracts and insert some of your own creativity into the brewing process.

Malt extracts of all kinds are widely available from home-brew stores and online retailers. *You will find a list of some of these retailers in the resource section at the back of this book.* If you begin your home-brewing adventure using a prepackaged home-brew kit, you will probably be using a malt extract.

Hops

Hops serve several purposes in the brewing of beer. Hops flavor beer, give it a particular aroma, and act as a preservative. Hops are available to home brewers in two forms: whole and pellet. Whole hops are completely unprocessed, and pullets are pulverized hop

Hops in pellet form

flowers processed to resemble gerbil food. Whether you use the whole or pellet form of the hop will become a matter of personal preference. Generally speaking, pellets are available to the home brewer in a greater variety. Most home-brew stores will have pellets in airtight packages available to the consumer.

Hops, like malt, come in many different varieties. The name of the particular hop variety generally refers to the region or beer style that it is associated with. The United States Department of Agriculture lists about 175 different varieties of hops that are grown in the U.S. Hops, like any other crop, vary from geographical location to geographical location. They are as varied as the climates, soils, and other geographic variables they originate from.

When home brewers consider the hops they will use in any particular brew, they generally consider three things, or three purposes they will ask of the hops: bittering, flavoring, and aroma.

Hop resins determine what part the hop will play in the brewed beer. Hops contain two types of acidic resins that affect the taste and aroma of the beer they are used in. Alpha acids affect the bitterness and flavor of beer, while beta acids affect the aroma of the beer.

Brew Note: As you proceed in your learning, you will encounter the abbreviation IBU. IBU stands for international bitterness units. This number indicates the bitterness of a particular beer, a bitterness brought about by the hops. An IBU is measured using of a spectrophotometer and solvent extraction. A dark wheat beer with a low hop profile might have an IBU as low as 10 to 15 while an India pale ale may have an IBU of 110 and a double India pale ale as high as 200. At the 2007 Copenhagen Beer Festival, an experimental brew called "Mikkeller X Hop Juice" had an IBU of 2007!

Hops used for bittering and flavoring are added to the wort at the beginning of the boiling procedure. The boiling wort isomerizes the alpha acid of the hops. **Isomerize** means the heat causes a chemical reaction in the hops that releases the bitter flavor. The heat does not isomerize beta acids.

Hops used for aroma are added at the end of the boil or after the wort has cooled and just before fermentation. Adding hops after the boil is called **dry hopping**.

Common hops

Some of the more common hop varieties include the following (hop notes and descriptions provided by the USDA):

Cascade — Used as an aroma hop in certain brewery blends. Cascade hops are low in bitterness and popular.

Chinook — A high-alpha/aroma hop primarily for bitterness addition. They are adapted to Oregon, Washington, and Idaho but grown now mostly in Washington. Considered a super-alpha hop by the trade, these super-alpha hops have a high level of alpha-acids and are used as bittering agents in beer.

Cluster — A highly commercial variety of hop that has an average IBU.

Kent Goldings — An English hop variety that is widely used in British brews. This is, traditionally, an aroma hop.

Fuggles — Another popular English hop, it gives beer an earthy flavor. It was developed in Great Britain in the 19th century, and it has been grown commercially in Oregon since about 2000.

Hallertau — A German lager hop named after the Hallertau region of Bavaria, the largest hop planting area in the world. This hop is used, primarily, as a lager and pilsner aroma hop.

Mount Hood — Related to the Hallertau described above, this is a popular aroma hop. It is a good finishing hop for both lagers and ales.

Northern Brewer — This is referred to as a dual-purpose hop for its bittering qualities and its woody aroma. This hop is of English origin.

Perle — Another dual-purpose hop, though this one is of German origin. Perle hops have a fruity profile.

Saaz — A spicy pilsner hop that originates in the Czech Republic and is used as an aroma hop.

Spalt — An aroma hop from the Spalter region of Germany. This hop has a subtle spicy aroma.

Sterling — An American dual-purpose hop with a floral bouquet and a moderate IBU.

Styrians — An English dual-purpose hop that is appropriate for lagers and ales.

Tettnanger — A classic aroma hop from Germany, though often employed as a dual-use hop as well.

Willamette — Grown primarily in Oregon, this is a popular dual-use hop with a sweet aroma.

Brew Note: Noble hops are hop varieties that have been grown in Germany and the Czech Republic since about the 6th century A.D. Traditionally, the noble hops are said to be Hallertau Mittelfrueh, Tettnang Tettnanger, Spalt Spalter, and Czech Saaz. Those brewers that are less traditional would include the English hop varieties of Fuggles and East Kent Goldings and the Slovenian variant of Fuggles, known as Styrian Golding in the noble hop family, as well.

The table below lists some the more common hop varieties and the percentage of alpha acid that each variety contains. Those with the lower percentages are used as aroma hops and those with the higher percentages are bittering hops. The hops in the mid-range are dual-purpose and flavoring hops.

Hop Variety	Country of Origin	Alpha Acid %
Amarillo	U.S	8–11
Brewer's Gold	England	7–11
Cascade	U.S.	4.5–6
Chinook	U.S.	12–14
Cluster	U.S.	5.5–8.5
Columbus	U.S.	14–18
Crystal	U.S.	3.5–5.5
Fuggles	England	4–5.5
Goldings	England	4–5.5
Hallertau / Hallertauer Mittelfrüh	Germany	3.5–5.5
Hersbrucker	Germany	3–5.5
Horizon	U.S.	11–13
Mount Hood	U.S.	5–8
Newport	U.S.	10–17
Northdown	England	7.5–9.5
Northern Brewer	England	8–10
Nugget	U.S.	12–14
Perle	Germany	7–9
Polnischer Lublin	Poland	3–4.5
Saaz	Czech Republic	3–4.5
Simcoe	U.S.	12–14
Spalt	Germany	4–5
Sterling	U.S.	6–9
Strisselspalt	France	3–5
Styrian Goldings	Slovenia	4.5–6
Summit	U.S.	17–19
Target	England	9–12.5
Tettnanger	Germany	3.5–5.5
Vanguard	U.S.	5.5–6
Warrior	U.S.	15–17
Willamette	U.S.	4–6

As you start to create your own home brew, the hops you use in your beer will be determined by the style of beer you make. Some beer styles, such as India pale ales, are highly hopped and contain several types of hops to serve several purposes. Other beers, such as stouts, have low hop profiles. If you begin your brewing using a kit, they will provide you with the most appropriate hops for the particular beer you brew. As you gain experience and learn about the wonderful world of hops, you will begin to choose your hops to suit your own particular tastes.

Yeast

Yeast is a microorganism classified as a fungus. More than 1,500 species of yeast have been identified, and this number is estimated to be only 1 percent of the species of yeast in existence. Yeast is used for a variety of purposes such as baking and brewing. As with the other ingredients described here for brewing beer,

Brewers yeast

a large number of yeast strains are available for the brewer to use depending on the type of beer. You read in Chapter 1 about the history of brewing beer and the identification of yeast by the Dutch naturalist Anton van Leeuwenhoek in 1680. Before this time, yeast was used in the brewing of beer, but it was done as part of a natural process that was not fully understood by the brewers. Natural wild yeast strains from grains and fruit fed on the fermentable sugars in the grain and produced the CO_2 (carbon dioxide) and ethanol, the carbonation and alcohol, that makes beer.

Today, yeast cultures are grown in laboratories and made available to home brewers to make many different styles of beer. Although some strains of yeast are appropriate for wheat beers, others are more appropriate for lagers.

When brewers consider which yeast to use in the brewing of specific beers, there are a number of things to take into account that vary from yeast strain to yeast strain. Brewers will consider attenuation, flocculation, fermentation temperature, and alcohol tolerance of yeast to be used.

Fermentation occurs when yeast transforms sugar into carbon dioxide and ethanol. **Attenuation** refers to the percentage of sugar the yeast consumes to do this. A 100-percent attenuation would result in the final gravity (FG) of 1.000 or less. **Gravity** is defined here as the density (thickness) of a liquid relative to the density of water. When you first mix your brew's ingredients together, the density is higher than it will be after the yeast has transformed the sugars into carbon dioxide and ethanol. For example, a beer with an original gravity (OG) of 1.050 and a final gravity of 1.012 would have a 73.07 percent apparent attenuation. Here is an equation for figuring apparent attenuation using specific gravity:

$$\% \text{ Apparent Attenuation} = (OG - FG / OG - 1) \times 100$$

Flocculation is a word that describes the yeast clumps that gather (flocculate) to form dregs at the bottom of the fermenter at the end of the fermentation cycle. Thus, the yeast can be gathered from the bottom of the fermenter and used for the next fermentation. Brewers will see that while some yeast has low to medium rates of flocculation, other yeast strains have high flocculation rates. Yeast is capable of amassing in three different ways for different purposes:

- Mating and DNA exchange
- Development and differentiation
- A survival strategy in unfavorable conditions

Fermentation temperature is another important component brewers look to when deciding which yeast strains to use to ferment their brews. Optimum fermentation temperatures range from 48 degrees F for some bottom-fermenting lager yeasts to 80 degrees F for a Belgian ale yeast.

Choosing the right yeast

Although beer drinkers might enjoy drinking alcohol, if they consume too much of it, it will do them harm. The same goes for yeast. A wide varity of yeast is available to brewers, and these different strains tolerate alcohol at varying levels, much like people do. As brewers decide which strains of yeast to use in their brew, alcohol tolerance is considered. When you shop for yeast, you will note that some yeast strains have low tolerance levels while other strains of yeast have medium or high alcohol tolerance levels. Brewers use

Vial of White Labs Yeast.
Photo courtesy of
www.KirksBrew.com

yeast that tolerates between 5 percent ABV (alcohol by volume) and 20 percent ABV. Few beers have an ABV of 20 percent. Most beers will range between 4 percent and 9 percent ABV. Most beer recipes will suggest a variety of yeast to use that is compatible with the beer you are going to brew.

Safeale dry ale yeast. Photo courtesy of www.KirksBrew.com

As you begin to brew beer, you probably will begin by using a kit that will have all of your ingredients pre-packed. The yeast already will be chosen to suit the style of beer you will be brewing. Note, however, as you brew your second and third batch using a kit that every style seems to have its own strain of yeast particular to that style of beer, and that observation is largely true. The next time you visit your local home-brew store, ask if they have any sales brochures for laboratories that produce yeast for breweries. In these brochures, you will see that yeast strains will have a product number and a name that refers to the style of beer they are appropriate for, such as German ale, American ale, or Munich lager. With each of these strains, you can ferment multiple specific beer styles within each of these broader categories. For example, with the yeast named American ale, you might brew American pale ale, American amber ale, India pale ale, stout, or any number of other beer styles. You might choose a yeast strain called Irish ale to brew stout, American amber ale, or a number of other beers. Choosing your yeast, like choosing your malts and hops, will become a matter of taste and creativity.

The question here might be: Is there a difference in the beer fermented by yeast named American ale and a yeast named Irish ale? The answer is yes. As you shop for yeast strains, you will notice some yeasts that might appear to be similar in nature will produce different characteristics in the final brew. American ale yeast might give the beer a citrus taste while British ale yeast might result in beer with a maltier profile.

As you advance in your brewing, you will learn the ins and outs of choosing and using yeast. You will learn which yeast strains give you the exact flavor in your favorite style of beer.

Brew Note: In brewer terminology, the adding of yeast into the wort for fermentation is called **pitching**. You also will come across the term "pitch rate" that notes the amount of yeast culture you will add to wort for fermentation. Most wort will require only a single pitch, which is generally how much you will get in a single package of yeast, either dry or liquid. If you plan to brew a batch of beer with an original gravity above 1.065 (such as a moderately high-gravity porter), you probably will need to double pitch. If your brew has an original gravity greater than 1.085 (such as a heavy imperial stout) you may have to triple pitch. The most economic way to do this is to build a starter culture from the yeast you have.

To build a starter culture:

1. If you are using a Wyeast liquid yeast, you will need to activate yeast pack 24 hours before continuing to step 2.

2. Heat 30 oz. of water to boil in a medium saucepan.

3. Add ½ lb. (about 1 ½ cups) of dry malt extract (DME) to boiling water.

4. Stir DME well to dissolve.

5. Boil DME for about 15 minutes.

6. After five minutes of boil, add ½ tsp. yeast nutrient (this is optional).

7. After 15 minutes of boiling, remove liquid (now wort) from heat.

8. Cool wort as quickly as possible by putting saucepan in a sink full of cold water.

9. When wort is about 75 degrees, pour it into a larger glass bottle (growler).

10. Add yeast to wort, and stir well.

11. Cap with an airlock.

12. Allow yeast mixture to sit at 70 degrees for 24 hours.

13. You now have a double-pitch quantity yeast starter.

Yeast is a living organism. If you care for your yeast, you will be able to keep it alive and reuse the yeast that remains in your primary fermenter once it has done its job. Yes, the yeast will continue to live and be active. The yeast will not be able to work for you in perpetuity, but you will be able to get three or four good batches of brew from a single batch of yeast if you keep your brew and equipment in good, clean order. If you choose to repitch your yeast, it is vital that all of the equipment and area you work in are completely sanitary. If you work in unsanitary environments with unsanitary equipment, you risk losing an entire batch of beer.

There are several ways to reuse yeast from a batch of beer. The manner in which you maintain the yeast will be determined by when you plan to reuse it. If you plan to repitch your yeast immediately, you can take the following steps:

1. Plan to harvest the yeast immediately after you transfer your brew from the primary fermenter into a secondary fermenter or into a bottling bucket.

2. Clean and sanitize a quart glass jar and lid.

3. Clean and sanitize the neck of the primary fermenter.

4. Pour 1 quart of yeast sludge from the fermenter into the jar, and cap the jar loosely.

5. Clean out the primary fermenter, and pour the quart of yeast solution back into the primary fermenter.

6. Pour a fresh batch of wort directly into the fermenter on top of the yeast.

7. Aerate, and continue as usual.

If you do not plan to use the yeast immediately, you can follow the direction above to step 5 and then store the yeast in the refrigerator for up to one week.

If the brewing process fascinates you, you will grow more fascinated the more you learn about yeast and how they act to ferment your brew. The information in this section is just the tip of the iceberg that is yeast and fermentation. There will be more about yeast as you progress through this book and into intermediate and advanced brewing procedures.

Water

Water is, perhaps, the most overlooked ingredient in the brewing process. You will remember, though, that beer is made up of 95 percent water. Given this statistic, it could be argued that water is the most important component of brewing beer. You, as a home brewer, should examine a number of factors when you decide whether to use your home tap water for brewing. Know how hard or soft your water is, and have a feel for the general taste of your water.

A good place to start to get a feel for the quality of your water is to do a pH test. According to the Environmental Protection Agency, "The pH scale measures how acidic or basic a substance is. It ranges from 0 to 14. A pH of 7 is neutral. A pH less than 7 is acidic, and a pH greater than 7 is basic. Each whole pH value below 7 is ten times more acidic than the next higher value. For example, a pH of 4 is ten times more acidic than a pH of 5 and 100 times (ten times ten) more acidic than a pH of 6. The same holds true for pH values above 7, each of which is ten times more alkaline — another way to say basic — than the next lower whole value. For example, a pH of 10 is ten times more alkaline than a pH of 9.

"Pure water is neutral, with a pH of 7.0. When chemicals are mixed with water, the mixture can become either acidic or basic. Vinegar and lemon juice are acidic substances, while laundry detergents and ammonia are basic." You can purchase pH test kits at most large hardware stores.

You also might want to know how hard your water is. Hard water is measured by the amount of mineral salts that exist in it. You can get a report on the hardness of your home's water from your municipal water service. Also, you can get test kits at your local hardware store that will test your water. You will see on the table below numbers that correspond to the water's alkalinity and hardness.

Needless to say, you probably want to start with water that is as close to neutral as possible. If you are really curious to find out about the state of the water you are using from your tap, you probably can go to your city's municipal website and search for a water quality report issued by your local water system. The sidebar to the right has information included in an annual water report submitted by the City of Lincoln, Nebraska. The

Water Quality Parameters

pH (in pH units) 7.71

Total Alkalinity (CaCO) 3 160 ppm
Total Hardness (CaCO) 3200 ppm
(12 grains per gallon)
Total Dissolved Solids 336 ppm
Calcium 54.4 ppm
Chloride 20.5 ppm
Iron <0.05 ppm
Manganese 1.04 ppb
Sodium 30.6 ppm
Sulfate 77 ppm
(12/10/09)

Lincoln's water is moderately hard.
Alkalinity, pH and hardness are important if considering a water softener.

report also offers the note at the end that "Lincoln's water is moderately hard." This is good to know.

Of the items listed in the water report above, six will have the greatest impact on brewing: carbonate (noted on the above table as total alkalinity), chloride, sodium, calcium, sulfate, and magnesium.

On a water report, you often will see these items listed in parts per million (ppm), which is equivalent to 1 milligram per liter (mg/L). To convert the ppm listed on your local water report to mg/L, you can go to **www.unitconversion.org/concentration-solution/part-per-million-ppm-conversion.html**. This website, UnitConversion.org, provides many online conversion tools and resources.

Carbonate and bicarbonate (CO3 and HCO3)

Carbonate is probably the most vital ion for all grain brewing. The total alkalinity of the brew water will affect the acidity of the mash. If alkalinity levels are too low, the mash will be too acidic, especially when using darker malts (which have higher acidity). If alkalinity is too high, mash efficiency will suffer. This means that you will not realize the amount of malt sugar you should. Recommended alkalinity levels are 25-50 mg/l for pale beers and 100-300 mg/l for darker beers.

Chloride (Cl)

Chloride also improves the body of the brew in low concentrations. Heavily chlorinated water should be avoided as it will affect the fermentation of the yeast and will give your beer chlorine-like flavors and aromas. Normal brewing levels should be under 150 mg/l and not exceed 200 mg/l. If your water is heavily chlorinated, you can reduce the chlorination by using a carbon filter. You also can reduce chlorination by boiling the water for 20 to 30 minutes before use or by drawing your water 24 to 48 hours before you use it and allowing it to sit in an open pot.

Sodium (Na)

Sodium gives body to beer. Excessive sodium, on the other hand, will make your beer taste like salt. If you have high-sodium water, it might be because you have a household water softener. It is suggested that you do not brew with water that has gone through a household water softener. Sodium levels in the 10 to 70 mg/l range are normal, and levels of up to 150 mg/l can enhance malty body and fullness, but levels over 200 mg/l should be avoided.

Calcium (Ca)

Calcium affects the brewing process in many ways. Calcium lowers the wort pH during the mash cycle and is a vital yeast nutrient. It is a good thing to have calcium levels in the 100 mg/l range. Calcium additives should be considered if your water profile has calcium levels below 50 mg/l. The range 50mg/l to 150 mg/l is preferred for brewing.

Sulfate (SO4)

The amount of sulfate in your local water will have an affect on hop bitterness and the IBU readings you get from your final product. Sulfate adds a dry and sharp character to highly hopped brews. Sulfate will also reduce the pH of your mash, but not as much as carbonates will because sulfate has a lower alkalinity than carbonates. Elevated sulfate levels will give your brew an overly sharp and unpleasant taste. Normal levels are 10-50 mg/l for pilsners and light beers and 30-70 mg for most ales. Other beers, especially pale ales, will require higher levels.

Magnesium (Mg)

In measured amounts, magnesium is a vital yeast nutrient. Levels in the 10-30 mg/l range are desirable, primarily to aid yeast. Levels above 30 mg/l will give a dry, sharp, or bitter taste to the beer.

Adjusting Your Water

Local tap water can be diluted with purified or distilled water to adjust your target water profile. Also, you can use additives to increase the level of key minerals. Additives of choice are baking soda ($NaHCO_3$), table salt (NaCl), gypsum ($CaSO_4$), calcium chloride (CaCl), Epsom salts ($MgSO_4$), and chalk ($CaCO_3$).

Adjusting the hardness and pH of your water for brewing the perfect beer is a complicated matter, but it is good to know the state of your water. For beginning brewers, if you have water that falls way outside the range of neutral in pH, hardness, and/or taste, you might consider brewing with neutral purified or spring water. The cost of 5 gallons of water is not prohibitive, and you will be much more assured and happy with the results you will achieve rather than the ones you will achieve with unsatisfactory water.

Additional Ingredients

The ingredients described above come under the heading "Necessary Ingredients" and are those ingredients described in the German Beer Purity Law. Malted barley. Hops. Yeast. Water. Basic beer. Depending on how you prepare these basic ingredients and the wide variety of malts, hops, yeast, and water available to you, you can make a wide variety of beer. However, adjunct ingredients also can be used in your brew to achieve a wide variety of goals from flavoring your brew, to aiding your yeast's propagation, to clarifying agents. Various sugars are employed as priming agents when beer is bottled. Other grains such as rice, corn, and rye are used as starch adjuncts to aid the fermentation and achieve other goals such as adding body to the brew or to increase the alcohol content. The list below will describe some common brewing adjuncts and their purposes.

Note that when it comes to flavoring adjuncts, you are only limited by your own creativity. Flavoring adjuncts range from chili peppers to vanilla. A few common flavoring adjuncts will be described here, but as you learn the art and craft of brewing, feel free to create your own unique flavor sensations.

Starches

Wheat — Wheat is, perhaps, the most common adjunct used in brewing beer. Wheat and its use have been described earlier in this book, not as an adjunct but as a primary ingredient. This testifies to its common usage in brewing beer. Wheat is a grain, like barley, though its husk is not as fibrous as barley. The fibrous nature of barley is vital in the sparging stage of brewing when the grain is rinsed. Wheat also is not as rich in amylase as barley. Amylase is a digestive enzyme that aids in the conversion of starch into sugars.

What wheat does bring to beer is flavor. Most wheat beers are brewed with at least 25 percent wheat, and many have a higher percentage of wheat in them. Wheat beer is often noted for its "sour" flavor, much like the sourness of sourdough bread.

Rye — Malted rye is used in brewing in much the same way as wheat. Rye, like barley and wheat, is a cereal grain. Its use in brewing is not as common as wheat, but when used, it produces similar results. Like wheat, when beer is brewed with rye as an adjunct, the product will be of a sour character. A style of rye beer brewed in Bavaria uses 60 percent malted rye. This brew is known as roggenbier. Roggenbier is similar in nature to the German hefeweizen.

Corn — Corn has a subtle flavor when used in brewing, but it does offer beer the flavor of corn. Corn is used, primarily, to increase alcohol production in beer. When it is used in this manner, it is used as corn syrup, which is highly fermentable. Because it is cheaper than many other grains, major commercial brewers quite often use corn to increase the alcohol content in products such as malt liquor.

Rice — Rice has a subtler flavor than corn does and is used to increase the alcohol content. Rice offers a dryer flavor than corn that can accentuate the bitter flavor of the hops.

Oats — Oats will lend a particular creaminess to a brew. If you have ever enjoyed oatmeal stout, you know it is smoother than standard stouts. Oats make up about 20 percent of the grains in oatmeal stout. They have high oil and fat content compared to barley. It is this content that contributes to the creaminess of the final brew.

Many other grains may be used as adjuncts in the brewing process. Sorghum is a grain that is quite common in Africa and often used in the brewing process there. Wild rice is a grain native to the northern Midwest in the United States and has been used to give a nutty flavor to beer. Buckwheat, millet, and quinoa are also more unusual to the brewing process, but as you learn and begin to experiment, you might want to try these grains.

Sugars

During the mashing process, grains — mostly malted barley — are steeped in hot water to convert stored starch into a fermentable sugar. When you engage in extract brewing, which is where you will probably begin as a home brewer, this step has already been done for you. When you look at a recipe for extract brewing, you will see ingredients that are referred to as "fermentables." Fermentables are either liquid malt extract (LME) or dry malt extract (DME). These extracts are malts that already have been converted into fermentable sugars.

You often will come across recipes that call for additional sugars to assist in fermentation. You also, more than likely, will employ sugar when bottling to assist in carbonation. This sugar is called priming sugar.

Sugars used in the brewing process generally fall into four categories:

- Starch sugar
- Cane sugar (sucrose)
- Lactose (milk sugar)
- Honey

Starch sugar — The starch sugars are the most common brewing adjunct as they are the most closely related to the sugars in DME and LME. Indeed, malt extracts and the wort created during mashing is a starch sugar.

If you are a beginning brewer using a kit obtained at a local brew shop or via mail order, you might find an ingredient called maltodextrin listed as a fermentable. In many recipes, maltodextrin will be added to your brew at the same time as the LME or DME. Maltodextrin is only slightly fermentable and is listed as such, though you might see many notes as you read about ingredients that say it is not fermentable.

Maltodextrin is a starch sugar often made from corn, rice, or potato starch. The starch is cooked down, and a simple white powder is produced. This white powder that resembles confectioners' sugar is maltodextrin. Maltodextrin, when used, can add body and smoothness to beer that is low in malt.

Cane sugar — Cane sugar is the sugar that comes from sugar cane and, less often, sugar beets, sorghum, or sugar maple. Although maltodextrin is only slightly fermentable and nearly tasteless, most of the cane sugars are highly fermentable, and each of them has their own particular flavor. If you wander the craft beer aisles of your local beer retailer, you will see a variety of beers that are flavored with sorghum, maple syrup, and several other forms of cane sugar.

Fresh raw sugar cane split in half

If you choose to employ cane sugar as a brewing adjunct, do so sparingly. For a 5-gallon batch of beer, start with no more than a pound of this type of sugar. Less than a pound is highly recommended. For some of these sugars, such as molasses or treacle, be aware that they will strongly affect the taste of your brew.

Lactose — Lactose is a non-fermentable sugar used to add body and flavor to brews such as stout and porter. It is milk sugar and will give your brew the sweet, smooth, creamy body you find in these dark brews.

Honey — Honey is fermentable and, like molasses, should be used sparingly to aid fermentation and give your beer a sweet, smooth flavor. The exact flavor that honey gives your brew depends on the type of honey you choose. Before you employ honey as an adjunct, become familiar with the differences in the various types of honey such as clover, alfalfa, orange blossom, or the dozens of other types available.

Flavorings

The way in which you choose to flavor your beer is limited only by your creativity. Early in this book, you read a recipe for a pumpkin brew. Pumpkin brew has become a popular fall favorite with many home and microbrewers. Beers  can be found flavored with spices, herbs, fruits, and vegetables. After you become acquainted with the basics of brewing and have a couple of batches under your belt, you might want to consider a batch brewed with jalapeños, blueberries, or ginger.

As you consider various flavorings for your brew, talk to brewers that have been there before you. Research recipes that explore similar taste directions, but do not be afraid to chart new courses. You might just discover the latest taste sensation. Who says you cannot brew beer with celery and sage? It might be the perfect compliment to that Thanksgiving turkey.

The flavors listed below are only the tip of the iceberg and have been gleaned from microbrewers and home brewers across the country.

Fruits

Fruit is a popular choice as an adjunct flavor for beer. Many commercial microbrewers and major breweries produce beers flavored with a variety of fruit. Bud Light Lime is a widely marketed beer. This a light lager style  beer flavored with lime to add to the refreshing taste. Other fruit you might find flavoring the beers on your local retailers shelves are cherry, lemon, pumpkin, and peach.

When adding fruit to your beer, you have several options to consider, depending on how pronounced you want your fruit flavor to be. You can choose to add the fruit before primary fermentation if you want a subtler flavor, or you can add fruit during a secondary fermentation for a more robust fruit taste.

To include fruit in the primary (first) fermentation stage, add the fruit to the brew pot once the boil is done and before cooling the wort. Be sure to do a good job of cleaning the fruit and removing all seeds or pits. After the fruit has been cleaned, mash it with a food processor. It does not have to be mashed super smooth, just roughly mashed. As your wort reaches 200 degrees, add the fruit pulp, and cover the pot. If you add the fruit when the wort is more than 200 degrees, you will release the pectin in the fruit, and this will cause your final brew to have a haze. Let the wort rest for 20 minutes. Check the temperature of the wort after ten minutes; you want it to be between 200 and 160 degrees. If your wort is less than 160 degrees, return the pot to a low heat and careful bring the temperature back to about 180 degrees. Watch the heat carefully. After 20 minutes, you can chill the wort as quickly as possible with a wort chiller or by placing the pot in a sink full of ice. You then will proceed to ferment the brew as you normally would but allow the pulp to remain in the brew during the primary fermentation. After fermentation has slowed considerably, but not stopped, you can transfer the brew to a secondary fermenter, leaving the pulp behind.

If you want a bolder fruit flavor in your brew, you can add the fruit during a secondary fermentation stage. To do this, clean the fruit and remove seeds and pits. Process the fruit to a finely mashed pulp. You might need to add a little water if the fruit is not particularly juicy. Put the mashed pulp in a saucepan and heat it to 180 degrees, stirring constantly. Allow it to be at 180 degrees for five minutes. Remove the fruit from the heat, cover it, and allow it to sit for 20 minutes. After the 20-minute rest, cool the fruit quickly, and add it to the secondary fermenter before you transfer your beer from the primary fermenter to the secondary fermenter. Allow the brew to sit in the secondary fermenter with the fruit for at least two weeks before bottling.

Vegetables

Although vegetables might not be as popular as fruits for flavoring beer, a number of vegetables frequent the microbrew aisles of your local retailer. Vegetable-flavored beers are much harder to come by than those flavored with fruit. For those of you that revel in experimentation, this may be an area to explore as you consider beer competitions and ways to get your daily requirement of six servings of veggies.

Exploration of the microbrew market will discover beers flavored with hot peppers such as jalapeños and habeneros. You may also come across beers flavored with tomato and spices in the manner of a bloody mary.

Flavor your brew with vegetables in the same manner that you would with fruits. Follow the directions given above for fruit.

Spices, Herbs, Roots, and Other Flavors

You can add other flavors to your brew on their own, or you can add them to compliment a fruit or vegetable you have added. You might choose to add cinnamon on its own or go for the pumpkin pie flavor of pumpkin, cinnamon, and maybe a little nutmeg. Again, the flavorings you choose are only limited by your own palate and creativity. Some of the more common flavorings to beer include:

- Allspice
- Anise
- Cacao
- Cardamom
- Cinnamon
- Clove
- Coriander
- Ginger
- Heather
- Juniper berries or boughs
- Licorice
- Nutmeg
- Orange or lemon peel
- Sarsparilla
- Spruce needles or twigs (see spruce beer)
- Wintergreen
- Wormwood
- Yarrow

Many of the flavorings listed above, as well as fruit flavorings, can be purchased as extracts or as liquid flavorings from brewer supply stores and online retailers.

CASE STUDY:
BEN BATTEN

I've been brewing for my friends and myself for just more than two years. I brew styles I like to drink and try new things. I have entered my beers into the state fair for judging, and last year I got third place in the IPAs. I also grow my own hops and harvest them for beer making.

I got started brewing when I tasted the beer a friend was brewing. He was also a new home brewer. I was surprised at how good it was compared to commercial craft beer. It is purely a hobby at this point, though I dream of making it a career. The creative process for me is the most enjoyable. And then, of course, you can enjoy drinking your own product. You can make a beer a million different ways and tweak it down to what you like. So many options are available. If it turns out, it makes you very happy.

The hardest thing about brewing beer is the patience needed. New brewers need to understand that they must take it slowly and not push too much. I consider my beer successful if it looks, smells, and tastes like a beer I want to drink.

I like to find a clone recipe for a commercial craft beer that I really like and then change it just a little bit so I am not copying the brewer exactly. One tip: Always use more hops. My favorite beer to brew is IPA. My favorite beers to drink are IPA and double IPAs.

I think two important things that new brewers can use to be more successful are keeping fermentation temperature down on ales in the lower to mid-60s if possible. Also, rapid cooling of hot wort and wort aeration will help. Cleanliness is also important.

Words of wisdom I have to pass on to those who are just getting started in brewing beer are: Have fun with it; it's your own product. Experiment and enjoy the process. I don't see myself ever giving this hobby up.

Shopping for Ingredients

Having just read about various types of malted grains, varietal hops from around the world, and yeasts that you cannot find in the baking aisles of your local grocery store, you are probably wondering, "Where can I get this stuff?" The best place to start your shopping is at a local BYO (brew your own) shop. Brew your own is not the commercial name of a particular store, but the acronym embraced by the movement of home brewers. The advantage of starting your shopping at a local retailer is that they are a wonderful source of information about everything home brewing.

A good example of a local home-brewing supply retailer is Kirk's Brew in Lincoln, Nebraska. Kirk's Brew has been in business since 1993, and Kirk has been home brewing since 1982. With nearly 30 years of home-brewing experience under his belt, Kirk is a great source of informative home brew tips and knowledge.

Like many home-brew supply retailers, Kirk's Brew sells through his storefront as well as via his website (**www.kirksbrew.com**). There is a long list of home-brew retailers in the resource section at the back of this book.

Another great source of information regarding ingredients and supplies is *Brew Your Own*, The How-To Homebrew Magazine. *Brew Your Own* is published eight times a year and is filled with product and ingredient reviews, recipes, tips, and the latest up-to-date information on the art and craft of home brewing (**www.byo.com**).

CASE STUDY: KIRK'S BREW

Kirk Weidner
www.kirksbrew.com

I currently brew beer at home at the intermediate level; that is malt extracts with specialty grains. I started a self-study of beer in 1982 that led me to home brewing in 1983. What I enjoy most about home brewing is sampling the finished product. It's the most self-rewarding thing anyone could do.

The hardest thing about brewing beer is the patience required and taking your time with the brewing session. It is also difficult to wait for the beer to mature in the keg or the bottle.

I like to brew all styles of beer. There is no particular beer style I enjoy brewing more than the others. My favorite beer to drink changes from year to year. Porters, pilsners, and pale ales are some of my favorites.

Mistakes that are common to beginning brewers are worrying too much and either overdoing or underdoing the sanitizer. My words of wisdom to those who are just getting started in brewing beer? Relax. Don't worry. Be patient.

Chapter 4:
The Necessary Equipment

Technically, all you really need to brew a batch of beer is a pot to cook your ingredients in and a bucket or some other vessel in which to ferment your brew. When you buy a beginner home-brew setup, you will not get the cookpot, but you will get several fermentation buckets. Depending on the setup you purchase, you might even get a 5-gallon carboy. A **carboy** is a large bottle, the type you are used to seeing on office water coolers. Beginner brewing setups also might include some siphon hose, a siphon, a large thermometer, a hydrometer, a bottling bucket, and a bottle capper. With this equipment and your ingredients, you will be all ready to make your first batch of beer.

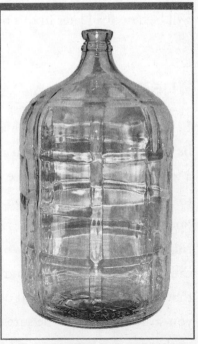

5-gallon glass carboy. Photo courtesy of www.KirksBrew.com

The equipment noted above is considered a good basic starting place to begin brewing. You can get a serviceable starter kit for about $80. You can get "ultimate" starter kits for $400. Several kits available fall between these extremes. If you are brand new to brewing and want to stick your toe in the water with a basic starter equipment kit and a basic ingredient kit, you can pay $80 for the basic equipment and $30 to $60 for an ingredient kit, depending on the style of beer you would like to brew.

This chapter will explain the basic equipment you will need and the equipment you might expect to find in a beginner's beer-making kit. Equipment beyond these basic kits that will make your brewing experience a little simpler also will be described. Advanced equipment will be described later in this book.

Where to Brew

Before diving into an examination of the equipment basics, it might be best to look at where you might consider brewing. Brewing needs a heat source (stove), a source of running water, and a cool dark place to allow proper fermentation. Many new home brewers begin their operations in their kitchens. This is a fine place to start, but you might run up a little resistance from others you share space with. Brewing beer can consume an entire day and does tend to produce an odor that those that do not enjoy beer might object to. If you plan to brew in a kitchen you share with others, be sure that you have a good ventilation system or that you can brew at a time when you can have a few windows open.

If you are brewing in your kitchen, be sure your sink is large enough to handle a large brew pot. After you are done cooking your wort, you will need to cool it as quickly as possible. Unless you have a wort chiller, you will need to get your pot into a large sink full of cold water and/or ice. If you do have a wort chiller, you will need to have a way to connect it to a water supply.

After you have prepared your beer to the fermentation stage, you will need a place for it to ferment. A cool basement is a good place for such activity, but many people do not have basements. Many home brewers find a place in a closet or pantry for this fermentation stage. The only drawback to allowing your beer to ferment in a closet is that fermenters have been known to explode. The explosions are due to overactive yeast with no place to go. Many home brewers will tell you stories about the time their imperial stouts blew out the airlock and exploded all over their hall closets. Another issue to consider in determining the best place to ferment your brew is, again, the smell. If you enjoy beer, the smell is wonderful. Those that do not enjoy beer find the smell unpleasant. When you choose a place to ferment, try to make it cool, out of the way, relatively well ventilated, and in such a location where if it does blow beer all over, you will not loose a large investment in dry cleaning.

As you gain experience, realize a growing interest in brewing, and start to acquire more equipment, you probably will want to find a place you can dedicate solely to brewing. Many home brewers move their operations in total to their garages or basements. Of course, to do this, you need a stove, running water, and, perhaps, a refrigerator in that location.

If you find that brewing beer is something you really want to pursue, you will make your brewing work wherever you may be. You will find that, whether it be creating beer recipes or designing the perfect brewing system, creativity is the key.

The Necessary Equipment

Given that you are set up with a stove, running water, and a cool dark place for your beer to ferment, you will need the following equipment pieces to get off to a good start.

You will remember reading about the history of brewing that the ancients brewed beer with little more than a big pot. You certainly can do this. You also can make your brewing experience a little easier by equipping yourself with the items described in this chapter. Beyond that, you also can spend thousands of dollars on an endless supply of brewing equipment with all the bells and whistles needed to outfit a large professional brewing operation. To get a good idea of what is possible, all you need to do is pick up a copy of *BYO* Magazine where you will see many ads for a wide array of brewing equipment. The potential is mind-boggling.

Photo courtesy of
www.KirksBrew.com

Pots — As you begin to make your beer, the first step in the process will call for you to steep your grains in several gallons of water. To complete this task, you will need a large 5- to 7-gallon pot, preferably stainless steel. You already might have a pot like this in your kitchen that you use to cook pasta or homemade chicken soup.

If you plan to add any flavorings such as fruit, you also will need a heavy-duty saucepan that accommodates a gallon or two. Again, a stainless steel pan is the best choice.

Steeping/straining bags — Most ingredient kits you buy will include a steeping bag to hold the grains you will steep. These bags generally are made of cotton and look like a large sock. You will be making what amounts to a large tea bag with this. If your ingredient kit does not contain a steeping bag, you can purchase muslin bags to serve this purpose from your local brew shop or from an online retailer.

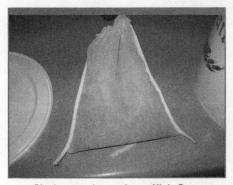

Photo courtesy of www.KirksBrew.com

Alternatively, you can make a bag from cheesecloth you purchase at your local grocery store. Be sure you tie it tightly at the top, or you will be straining a big pot of hot wort.

Some brewers have been known to use cotton socks and even nylon panty hose as steeping/straining bags. If you choose to go the nylon panty hose route, try not to let the nylon rest on the bottom of the pot, as the nylon might melt into your brew.

Spoons, stirrers, and paddles — You will be steeping large grain bags in several gallons of hot water, so you will need a large spoon or paddle to help you in this task. Many of the beginner equipment kits will include a large plastic stirring paddle. These paddles will be 18 to 24 inches long and look something like a canoe oar with holes on the bill. The good thing about these plastic paddles is that there is not a lot of heat transference up into the handle of the paddle. The downside of these tools is they are made of plastic, and there might be some concern of degradation over time.

If you have a long stainless steel spoon in your kitchen, or if you are concerned about plastic, go with the stainless steel. You can purchase a 21 to 24 inch stainless steel spoon for under $10 at a grocery store or an online retailer.

Brewing spoon and paddle. Photo courtesy of www.KirksBrew.com

Colander — Although a colander is not an absolute necessity, it is nice to have one to help drain your steeping bag. Also, some recipes will call for you to rinse your steeped grains, and a colander is great for this, especially if you have one that fits over the top of your brew pot. A large stainless steel or food-grade plastic colander is preferable, but because you will be placing steeped grain that is in a muslin or nylon bag, you can use just about any kind of sturdy colander. If your colander is strong enough to strain two pounds of cooked pasta, you can use it to drain steeped grain.

Thermometer — An instant-read food thermometer that ranges from 0 to 220 degrees F and can be inserted at least a couple of inches into the wort is desirable. "Instant read" means it indicates the temperature quickly, which is important when you are increasing or decreasing the heat of wort and you need to know exactly what the temperature is in an instant. You probably will find that two thermometers will come in handy, as it is good to know the temperature of your wort and the

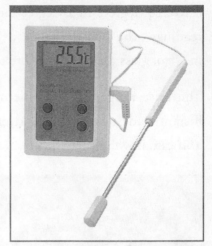

**Digital thermometer with probe.
Photo courtesy of www.KirksBrew.com**

temperature of water you might need to add to the wort. Often, you will find that one of your thermometers is not clean when you need it, so having a second thermometer will be useful. Also, you will find it useful if you have the kind of thermometers that can clip onto the edge of a pot. To test to see if your thermometers are accurate, boil some water and check the reading of the thermometer. If you get a reading of 212 degrees F, your tool is working properly.

A type of thermometer that you might come to appreciate is actually called a fermometer. A fermometer is a liquid crystal thermometer with a peel-off adhesive back you can stick on the sides of buckets or carboys while fermentation is in process. For this purpose, fermometers for home brewers range from 36 to 78 degrees in 2-degree increments.

Many home-brew equipment kits will include a long glass lab thermometer. These thermometers will offer a temperature range from

0 to 220 degrees in 2-degree increments. They also will give you fast readings. The one downside of these thermometers is that they are made of glass and are easily broken.

The price range for these thermometers is from about $3 for basic instant-read thermometers and fermometers to $7 for a lab thermometer. You can, however, pay much more for top-of-the-line instruments.

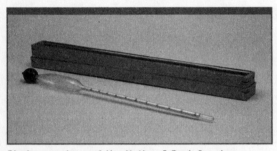

Photo courtesy of the National Park Service

Hydrometer — Most beginner home-brew equipment kits will include this instrument. A hydrometer is an instrument that measures the ratio of the density of the liquid, in this case beer, to the density of water. The number referred to is the specific gravity. When you start reading beer recipes, you will note that you will have an OG (original gravity) that is the density of the beer before fermentation. You also will have a FG (final gravity) that is the density of the beer after fermentation. The density of the beer will change as the yeast consume the sugars and transform them into gas (carbonation) and alcohol.

A hydrometer is a tool made of glass. It looks like a thermometer with a more bulbous end. The bulbous end is weighted with mercury or lead that allows the instrument to float vertically in liquid. When the hydrometer is lowered gently into the liquid, it floats freely with the weighted end down in the liquid. Hydrometers have a scale inside the stem. The point at which the surface of the liquid touches the stem of the hydrometer shows the number that reflects the gravity, or density, of the liquid.

You can calculate the ABV (alcohol by volume) of your brew using the OG and FG with this formula:

$$(OG - FG) \times 131 = ABV\%$$

*Note that all recipes and directions in this book refer to temperatures using the Fahrenheit scale.

Hydrometers are calibrated to give accurate readings when the liquid is at 59 degrees. The chance that your beer will be exactly 59 degrees when you take a hydrometer reading is slim, so there are several ways for you to find out what the gravity of your beer is. The table below shows approximate adjustments that can be made to your readings based on the temperature of your beer. When your beer is above 59 degrees, you add to the hydrometer readings and when your beer is less than 59 degrees, you will subtract from the reading. Remember, a hydrometer will show you the gravity of the liquid as compared to water, which has a gravity of 1.000.

Hydrometer Temperature Correction Table

Degrees Fahrenheit	Adjustment to Reading
40	- .0009
50	- .0006
59	CORRECT READING
72	+ .0013
80	+ .0026
90	+ .0041

100	+ .0061
110	+ .0081
120	+ .0106

Example: If you were to take a hydrometer reading when your beer was 100 degrees and you got a reading of 1.058, you would add .0061 to that number and find that your gravity was 1.0641. Readings are usually rounded to the closest third decimal place, so your gravity is 1.064.

You also can calculate the gravity of your beer using one of the several online calculators. The Beer Recipator website (**http://hbd.org/recipator**) has many great tools for the home brewer. The specific Web address for the hydrometer correction tool is **http://hbd.org/cgi-bin/recipator/recipator/hydrometer.html**.

Siphon — More specifically, the ideal tool is what is called a siphon racking cane. This tool allows you to draw liquid from one vessel to another. A siphon racking cane operates using a single stroke action that draws a siphon without disturbing sediment on the bottom of the delivering vessel. These canes are used when you transfer cooled wort from a cookpot to a fermenter and then from fermenter to a bottling bucket. Most canes have an attachment on the end that keeps sediment from being transferred along with the liquid.

Tubing — Food grade vinyl tubing is attached to the siphon described above or to the spigot of a bottling bucket. Six feet of tubing is an adequate length.

Fermenting vessel — When it comes to fermenting vessels, you have a number of different options. If you purchase a basic beginner's beer-making equipment kit, you will receive a fermenting bucket that has graduated marking to 5 gallons. The total capacity of the bucket will be 6 ½ gallons. These buckets, commonly referred to as "ale pales," are exactly what they sound like — big buckets — and are quite serviceable for beginning brewers. The tops of these buckets have small grommet holes where an airlock fits (see **airlock** below).

Photo courtesy of
www.KirksBrew.com

If you spend a little more money on a basic equipment kit, you will also receive a 5-gallon plastic carboy. A carboy is a large clear bottle, the kind you might see on a water cooler. The great thing about using a clear carboy to ferment your beer is you can watch the fermentation take place. It is an exciting show as the yeast become active and grow wildly for three or four days. The downside to using a carboy as a primary fermentation vessel is that they are somewhat difficult to clean.

If you choose to use a carboy as a fermentation vessel, you may want to invest $40 to $60 and get a glass carboy. Also, if you plan to go this route, you may want to get a 6-gallon carboy as opposed to the 5-gallon size. The larger size means you will be less likely to experience an active batch of beer that will burst out of the stopper of the smaller vessel.

Photo courtesy of
www.KirksBrew.com

Drilled rubber stopper — This particular drilled rubber stopper will fit into the opening at the top of the carboy. A hole drilled into the stopper accommodates an airlock.

Airlock — Airlocks are devices that allow gas to escape from a fermenting vessel but stop any outside air from entering. A standard airlock is a three-piece device. One piece is a tube that fits into the stopper or through a whole in the top of a fermenting bucket. The tube comes up from the inside of the vessel to the outside where it is surrounded by a small cup. The cup is filled halfway with water. A small cap is then placed over the tube. The cap covers the tube, but the bottom of this cap is submerged in water that has been placed in the cup. The result of this arrangement is that the tube that comes out of the bucket is placed in a bubble that is made up of water at the bottom and the plastic cap at the top. As gas is created in the fermenting bucket, it comes out of the tube. The rising gas pushes the cap up, and the gas is released through the water in the cup as a gas bubble. Because the tube is sealed off from the outside air, none can get in. An airlock is meant to keep outside air and bacteria out of fermenting brew where it could cause havoc. The third piece of this airlock is a cap that fits over the two described pieces.

A variety of devices are designed to achieve airlock. The device described above is probably the most common, and it is good for brews that ferment in the moderate to low range. Beer that is of a higher gravity

(1.065 and above) with the expectation of a more active fermentation period, such as stout, porter, and wheat beer, might require a blow-off hose (*check the next definition*) to get you through the primary fermentation period.

Blow-off hose — A blow-off hose is a hose of at least a half-inch in diameter that will fit snugly into the opening of a carboy. The larger diameter of the hose will allow greater blow-off of gas (CO_2) and krausen (the thick foam produced by yeast in the fermenting beer) during the primary fermentation period. Using an airlock rather than a blow-off hose in a brew that has an active fermentation could cause the airlock to become clogged and the fermenter to blow its lid. This will cause a huge mess for the home brewer.

Bottling bucket — You already have seen several mentions of this piece of equipment. A bottling bucket is much like the fermentation bucket described above with one exception: A hole is drilled on the side of the bucket near the bottom where a spigot is fitted. The spigot, capable of being opened and closed, allows liquid to flow out of the bucket. It can accommodate a length of tubing. After your beer is fermented, you will add priming sugar to the bottling bucket and then transfer the fermented beer to the bottling bucket.

Photo courtesy of
www.KirksBrew.com

Bottle filler — A bottle filler is a wand-type device that will attach to the end of the tubing that runs away from your bottling bucket. The bottle filler is placed in a bottle to touch the bottom of the bottle. When the filler touches the bottom of the bottle, a valve is pushed in that allows beer to flow from the bottling bucket to the bottle. When the bottle is filled, you simply lift the bottle filler, and beer stops flowing.

Bottles — You can buy bottles or you can save bottles you get from buying beer or soda. A couple of things to keep in mind if you plan to use bottles collected from your beer purchases:

- Bottles with pry-off caps are the ones to keep. Bottles that accommodate screw-off caps should be recycled. You cannot use screw-off caps.

- Brown, green, or colored bottled are better than clear bottles. Beer, yeast in particular, likes its shade.

- Bottles with flip-top caps, such as Grolsch bottles (these are generally 16-ounce bottles) are great to use.

A 5-gallon batch of beer will yield about two cases (48 bottles) of beer.

Some home brewers report that bottles known as P.E.T. (polyethylene terephthalate) bottles will work for home brewing. P.E.T. bottles are the 16-ounce plastic bottles that many types of soda come in. Glass is favored, though, as the P.E.T. bottles seem to have some effect on the taste of the beer. The upside to using P.E.T. bottles is that they have screw caps, and a bottle capper is not needed when bottling the beer.

Caps — You must use crimp-type caps that need to be pried off if you are using the flip-topped bottles noted above. Caps can be purchased at your local home-brew shop or from an online retailer. Caps cost about $4 for 144 (a gross) caps.

As mentioned above, you might choose to employ P.E.T. bottles, in which case you will need to use the screw caps that accommodate these bottles. P.E.T. caps sell for about $5 for 24 caps. To be safe, though, it is suggested that you travel the well-known path of standard crimp-type bottles and caps to start with.

Bottle capper — Several varieties of bottle cappers are available to the home brewer. If you begin by purchasing a standard home-brew equipment kit, you will receive a hand capper. A hand capper is a tool that is used to crimp caps on the top of beer bottles. They are easy to use but do take a little strength and coordination.

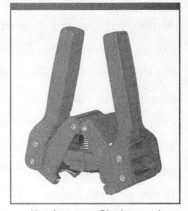

Hand capper. Photo courtesy of www.KirksBrew.com

Handcapper, caps and bottle brush. Photos courtesy of www.KirksBrew.com

Alternatively, you might choose to use a bench capper. This tool performs the same function as the hand capper but is designed for use on a bench or tabletop.

The equipment described here, except for the bottles and caps, is what you will receive in most basic home-brew equipment kits. Not all kits will include all of the equipment, and some kits might include one or two more pieces such as bottlebrushes and cleaners.

Also, many other types of equipment are available to the home brewer that will be described in coming chapters. This advanced equipment is the type that will be used to perform more advanced home-brewing procedures. However, with the equipment described here and the ingredients described in the previous chapter, you are well stocked to make your first batch of beer.

Kegs — An alternative to bottling your beer is putting it into a keg. Although there are a number of different types of kegs the home brewer can use, the most popular type of keg is the one known as the "corny" keg. These kegs are so called because a company called The Cornelius Company in Minnesota developed them. The corny kegs are a good choice for home brewers because they are small relative to the barrel kegs. Corny kegs are those you might associate with soft drinks. A good choice for the home brewer would be the 5-gallon corny keg. If you plan to keg your beer, you also will need the following pieces of equipment:

- CO_2 tank
- Dual gauge pressure regulator
- Two hoses (gas and beer)

You can purchase complete kegging systems that will have everything you need to get started from your local home-brew shop for a little less than $200. After you purchase the system, you will need to fill your CO_2 tank, which you can do at a beverage supply outlet in your area.

CASE STUDY:
DAREN YU

I would call myself an active home brewer. I enjoy studying the science behind it, but I especially like the end product and knowing that I'm getting something out of the hard work I put into it. I have several resources for learning about home brewing that I consult on a regular basis, as well as fellow home brewers. On Beeradvocate™ (**http://beeradvocate.com**), I'm fairly active in the home-brewing forum with answering questions about brewing and whatnot.

I became involved in home brewing by just talking with friends. A few of us were hanging out one day drinking various beers, and we began talking about breweries. Someone mentioned it would be cool to make our own beer, and something just clicked. I went and did some research on the process and different kits we could use. Coming from a rather heavy science background, learning about the chemistry and process intrigued me.

I've brewed for about three years, although I've been brewing much less recently due to school obligations. I brew as a hobby. I haven't read too much on the legal aspects of home brewing, but I do know certain states have laws against home brewing altogether, while other states have restrictions on the quantity you're able to brew. And of course, selling alcohol without a license is a big no-no. There are so many legal issues with alcohol, but for most home brewers, it's not a huge issue because we just brew for our own enjoyment.

I enjoy the hard work involved, seeing the fruition of the work, and sharing it with other people. It's like anything in life, in my opinion. You put in the work to create something special, see it come to life, and share it with your family, friends, and peers. It sounds cliché, but it's true. It's just like the woodworker who builds tables and chairs or a musician who composes and plays a piece of music. It's the art behind it.

You can make brewing as easy or as difficult as you want it to be. It also depends a lot on your personality. I know people who think brewing is this magical and mystical process and are simply afraid to even start the process. Others need instructions and demonstrations for every single step of the brewing process. And yet others get frustrated because their beer doesn't come out exactly the way they want it. Many factors are involved in brewing, and every step can be a potential hardship depending on how you look at it. For me, the most difficult part of brewing is bottle conditioning the beer. This is because I'm one of those people who does not enjoy measuring anything, and bottle conditioning is a finicky step that requires rather precise measurements. Other than that, brewing beer isn't difficult. Just a few basic things are absolutely necessary; the rest is completely up to your imagination.

I don't consider a bad beer a failure as long as I gained something from it. Did I overcarbonate or undercarbonate? Are there flavors that don't mesh well? Did I add too much or too little of an ingredient? Did I ferment at the wrong temperature? Is my beer infected? If, after brewing and tasting the beer, I am able to pinpoint a flaw in my recipe and/or brewing process, then I consider it a success because I have learned from the experience. But as long as the beer ends up tasting good, then I consider that a success as well.

One of my favorite recipes was actually somewhat of a mistake that came out better than expected. A long story short, we were going to brew an English barley wine of about 12 percent ABV similar to Thomas Hardy's Ale. We decided to be crazy and make our own recipe. Our beer came out a lot lighter in color and body than expected and was slightly bland. So, I decided to freeze the entire batch and remove the ice, making what we called an "eisbarleywine." It's aged for one year with oak, bourbon, and port wine and makes for a wonderful after-dinner warmer with some nuts and chocolate.

Here's the recipe:

The Count's Christmas Ale
Ingredients:

7 ½ lbs. base malt (we used pale 2-row. but Maris Otter would be preferred)
2 lbs. crystal malt 60ºL
6 ⅗ lbs. Extra Light LME
3 oz. East Kent Goldings hops (full boil)
Wyeast 1968 cake

Instructions:

Mash grains at 152 degrees F for 45 to 60 minutes. Vorlauf* and sparge until you have 6.5 gallons of wort. Add LME and bring to boil. Once there's a steady, rolling boil, add hops. After boiling and chilling, our target OG of 1.110 was hit, and we had 5 gallons of wort. Pitch yeast. Allow to ferment at 65 degrees F for one month. At this point, the gravity reading had dropped to 1.020. Transfer to secondary and allow to condition for two months. Freeze the beer and extract the ice from it. This process is accomplished by placing the beer in an environment (a freezer or outside in the winter, that is well below freezing. The beer is slowly frozen, and as it freezes, you remove the ice crystals. What remains is what you continue with to the conditioning process. After extraction, the gravity was 1.042, and we had half the volume of beer. Let beer condition in tertiary for one year with 1 ounce oak chips, ¾ cup Evan Williams sour mash bourbon, and ¾ cup Widmer's Special Reserve Port Wine. Bottle the beer uncarbonated (still) and enjoy in a snifter.

Note — Vorlauf is a term used for the recirculation of the wort and sparge water until the wort runs clear.

That was our fourth batch of beer. If I were to brew something like that today using all extract and steeped grains, I would use the following ingredients:

Ingredients:

12 lbs. extra light DME
1 lb. crystal malt 60ºL
½ lb. crystal malt 120ºL
2 oz. Northern Brewer hops (60 minutes)
2 oz. East Kent Goldings hops (15 minutes)
Wyeast 1968

As far as brewing techniques are concerned, to me each technique is an additional tool that can be used during the brewing process. Some techniques are simply essential; you cannot brew properly without using them. Other techniques are helpful but not essential. They alter the process somehow and may impart certain characteristics to your beer. Or they might be simply timesavers and are used as shortcuts. Regardless, I think it's important to learn as many of these techniques as possible. Even if it doesn't help your brewing process, it helps you learn as a brewer. I try to learn as many techniques as possible, and then make changes to them as needed to fit my brewing system and brewing style. I will admit though, the smell of a hot mash of malt is quite nice, and that is probably one of my favorite steps when all-grain brewing. And I also will add that my least favorite technique is the cleanup.

My favorite beers to brew are stouts. You can do so much with them. You can fruit them, over-hop them, add liquors, make them huge and imperial, ice distill them, etc.... Of course, you can do that to anything you brew, but there is something about stouts that make them more receptive to crazy additions than most other beers.

I've been on a sour beer kick lately. These are, currently, my favorite beers to drink. I love anything Cantillon and Drie Fonteinen. But they have only recently overtaken my love for Russian imperial stouts. I don't care if it's 95 degrees F outside, give me a Ten Fidy.

What are a couple mistakes that are common to beginning brewers?

A few things I've noticed:

- Wanting to immediately get into brewing crazy beers. Most people prefer what I call the "stepping-stone method" (or the normal way) where you start simply and work your way up to the crazy stuff. Of course, some people like being thrown in the deep end, which is fine if you like working like that. I happen to enjoy that.

- Not watching the temperature. I think this is one of the most important parts of brewing. You have a decent range in which to err, but that range tends to be lower than room temperature. You have to remember that you aren't the one making the beer, the yeast are! If you don't make them comfortable, they're not going to make good tasting beer. Think of it this way: if you make it hot, you turn your fermentor into a hot sweatshop, and your yeast are going to get stinky sweat in your beer. Then, if you keep it too cold, they're going to go into hypothermia and fall asleep on you.

- Not learning how to use the hydrometer. This tells you whether your beer is done. For most people, it's the only way you can tell if your beer is done.

- Being impatient. Many of the instructions that come with beer kits will tell you that your beer will be ready in two weeks. Sure, it's done fermenting by then, and your beer might be drinkable, but there's a period after fermentation that allows the yeast to "clean up" after themselves. As a rule of thumb that I use, if the beer is 5 percent ABV or less, it should take one to two weeks to ferment out completely, then I'll give it another week to condition, then either keg it or bottle it. And when you bottle the beer, you have to give it anywhere from two weeks to a month for it to fully carbonate. For higher ABV beers, I'll commonly leave them alone for a month before checking up on them. Then, I'll either let it condition a bit after that in secondary, or bottle it and then let it sit a few months. But like I said, it depends on your brewing system and what you're brewing. Let the yeast tell you when your beer is done.

- Aluminum versus stainless steel. It really doesn't matter. Aluminum is lighter and cheaper, hence why I use it.

Some words of wisdom to those who are just getting started in brewing beer:

- Relax; don't worry; have a home brew (or a craft brew, if you don't have any home brew yet).

- If you are considering starting brewing, ask yourself these questions

  - Do you enjoy putting in effort and labor to create something unique?

  - Do you have patience to wait or to do trial and error?

  - Do you have the capital to obtain the equipment and ingredients to start brewing?

  - Do you have (or can you obtain) an environment suitable for fermentation?

  - Can you make soup from scratch? Because if you can do that, you can probably brew.

- If you are seriously considering brewing and want to get started, I suggest...

  - Read John Palmer's *How To Brew* (there is a free version online: **www.howtobrew.com**).

  - Get Charlie Papazian's *The Complete Joy of Homebrewing.*

  - See if there are any home brewers who will let you brew with them so you can see what the process is like.

  - Get a decent equipment kit. I suggest a kit from Midwest Homebrewing and Winemaking Supplies (**www.midwestsupplies.com**) that has buckets and Better Bottles (plastic carboys instead of glass)

  - Ask questions. I'm on Beeradvocate a lot, and many folks on the forum are happy to answer questions.

- If you're a beginner brewer...

  - It's better to oversanitize than undersanitize. With that said, however, beer is much hardier than most people think.

  - Get a big kettle if possible, at least 10 gallons. That way your IPAs will actually taste like IPAs.

  - Consider a wort chiller if you do full wort boils. It takes chilling down to 20 minutes or less.

  - Don't be afraid to go crazy and experiment, but make sure you can always answer the question "What should this ingredient do for my beer?" when you consider adding an ingredient.

  - Your hydrometer is your best friend. It tells you, "Hooray, your beer is ready!"

  - Patience, my young padawan.

Chapter 5:
Brewing for Beginners

Chapters 3 and 4 presented the basic ingredients and equipment necessary for you to get started on your way into the wonderful world of home brewing. Looking back to the material covered in Chapter 1 though, you might well guess that many of these ingredients and equipment just complicate the process. This is not the case. If you are new to brewing, getting started with the prepackaged kits available to the novice home brewer almost makes the process foolproof. All that you need to bring to the table is the ability to read, follow directions, and be patient. Patience, you will learn, might be the most important thing, as brewing takes time. Patience, you have read and will read more about in the case studies presented in this book, could be the most important ingredient in brewing. Keep this in mind as you proceed.

If you choose to begin your home-brewing experience by starting with an ingredient kit, you have many beer styles and kit styles to choose from. The simplest of kits are those that have hopped malt extracts and do not require any specialty grains. These kits can be found at many home-brew stores and through online retailers. Coopers Brewery, an Australian company, produces a variety of beer-in-a-can kits. These kits require little time and no steeping of specialty grains. Other companies such as Brewer's Best package premeasured ingredients that will include malt extract, specialty grains for steeping, hops, yeast, priming sugar, and any other ingredient specific to a style of beer. These kits give beginning brewers a good taste of the entire extract brewing experience. It is highly recommended that beginning brewers begin with a kit such as this. Many home-brew stores also put together their own versions of these beer recipe kits.

For those brewers that are a little more adventurous, the directions that follow will take you step-by-step through the brewing procedure. Couple these instructions with talking to those you know have done this before, and you will be "good to go."

What follows in this chapter is the brewing procedure. This chapter will walk you through brewing your first batch of beer using a liquid malt extract (LME) and/or a dry malt extract (DME). The chapter will examine the procedure based on a single recipe. The recipe chosen for this exploration is an American pale ale. This recipe was chosen because it involves all of the steps you might be asked to perform in the creation of beer. Some recipes will not include a secondary fermentation, and some will not require dry hopping. Both of these procedures will be described in this American pale ale recipe. This chapter will take you through the process explaining each of the following steps:

- Ensuring that your equipment is clean
- Preparing the ingredients
- Steeping the grains
- Adding the LME/DME
- The boil
- Adding the hops

- Adding adjunct ingredients
- The cooling
- Gravity measurement
- Pitching the yeast
- Fermentation
- Dry hopping
- Secondary fermentation
- Priming
- Bottling
- Conditioning
- Drinking

Ensuring your Equipment is Clean

Before you begin to prepare your ingredients, it is vital that your equipment is ready to go. This means that your equipment and the place you use to brew are clean. You want to make sure anything that comes into contact with your beer is clean and that the space in which you work is clean. The reason that cleanliness is so important is that any unwanted bacteria that get into your beer will grow and make your beer an undrinkable waste of your time and money. The message is to do your diligence and clean before you start so you do not have to toss it after you finish.

You can employ a number of products and methods of cleaning to achieve satisfactory results. You can choose to purchase cleaners and sanitizers from your local home-brew store, or you can use common household cleaners such as bleach.

If you choose to purchase cleaners and sanitizers from your local home-brew shop, you will have the option of buying a one-step product, or you might buy several products that are used one after the other. Whatever you choose will be a matter of personal preference.

The two goals are cleanliness and sanitation. Clean means any unwanted grime is removed from the equipment. This grime simply might be dust, but it also might be beer remaining in used bottles, dried yeast in fermenting buckets, or any household dirt that might have gotten onto your equipment since it was last used. Clean does not necessarily mean sanitary. Sanitary means that your equipment is free from bacteria and other infective matter.

Some products on the market will take care of both tasks, cleaning and sanitation in one step. Some home brewers do not like these products for a variety of reasons, such as the length of time it takes them to work and the feeling that a residue is left on the equipment.

The two-step products that do separate jobs of cleaning and then sanitizing are preferred by home brewers who feel they have greater control over the process. They feel that their equipment is cleaner.

It is recommended that you experiment with several products to see for yourself what works best for you. The goal is to ensure you are working with clean equipment.

You can use household bleach to clean and sanitize your equipment, especially your bottles and work surfaces, by diluting one to three tablespoons of bleach to each gallon of water. If you choose to use bleach, it is vital that you rinse it well. Also, it recommended that bleach not be used on stainless steel or aluminum.

Bottles, if not cared for immediately after they are used, can be somewhat difficult to clean. Rinse your bottles out as soon as possible after you use them. To clean them, soak them in hot water and the cleaner of your choice. Rinse the bottle and allow them to air dry. Allow them to air dry for several hours upside-down and then for 24 hours, to be sure all of the moisture is out of them. Once the inside of the bottle is completely dry, cover the opening with a piece of aluminum foil. Place the covered bottles in your oven and heat the oven to 350 degrees. Do not place the bottles in a preheated oven, as they might break. Heat the oven with the bottles in it. Maintain the 350-degree temperature for one hour. Turn the oven off, and allow the bottles to cool before removing them. Leave the aluminum foil caps on the bottles until you are ready to fill them with beer.

One more word about cleaning before proceeding: The timing of your cleaning should coincide with the various tasks involved in the brewing process. For instance, you will not need to clean your bottles on brew day, as you will not need clean bottles for three to five weeks. Clean your workspace and the equipment you need immediately first. Before you start, clean your cookpot, any spoons or paddles, and any pans you will be using. You can clean your fermentation bucket, siphon, and hose as you are boiling your wort.

Preparing the Ingredients

Now that your equipment is clean and sanitized, you are ready to get started with your first batch of beer. As mentioned at the beginning of this chapter, the steps to brewing a 5-gallon batch of American pale ale will be described and explained here. If you begin your experiment with brewing by purchasing an ingredient kit, the ingredients will be similar to those listed below. The ingredients for this beer are as follows:

(Note: the following recipe offers several alternative ingredients. If your local home-brew store does not have one suggested ingredient, you may substitute another)

- 6 ⅗ lbs. light liquid malt extract (LME) **or** 5 lbs. unhopped light dry malt extract (DME)
- ½ lb. dark crystal malt (120ºL) **or** 1 lb. caramel malt (20ºL)
- 1 oz. Cascade **or** Willamette hops (60-minute boil)
- ½ oz. Cascade **or** Willamette hops (30-minute boil)
- ½ oz. Cascade **or** Willamette hops (ten-minute boil)
- ½–1 oz. Cascade **or** Willamette hops (dry hop)
- Wyeast 1056 American ale yeast **or** White Labs WLP American Ale Yeast Blend
- Priming sugar

Examination of ingredients

The ingredients listed above are standard ingredients for this type of beer. If you were to purchase an ingredient kit to brew American pale ale, you would find these ingredients in it, along with brewing instructions and maybe a disposable steeping bag and some bottle caps.

- 6 ⅗ lbs. light liquid malt extract (LME) <u>or</u> 5 lbs. unhopped light dry malt extract (DME)

Malt and malt extracts were described in Chapter 3 of this book. Whether you use LME or DME will become a matter of preference and availability. It is possible to combine LME and DME. The reason that a larger quantity of LME is used as compared to the DME is that LME is about 20 percent water.

The malt extract is what is known as fermentable. The fermentables employed in extract brewing are what provide the fuel that the yeast consume to produce alcohol and carbon dioxide.

- ½ lb. dark crystal malt (120ºL) or 1 lb. caramel malt (20ºL)

This ingredient is what is known as a specialty grain in this extract beer recipe. The specialty grains will be steeped early on in your brewing procedure and will offer flavor and color to your brew.

The difference in the ingredients offered here gives you a choice dependent on your taste. The dark crystal malt will result in a darker brew with a slightly more roasted flavor, while the caramel malt will result in a somewhat lighter beer with a little bit of sweetness.

Brew Note: The L that you see in the description of the malts (120°L or 20°L) refers to the color of the malt. Degrees Lovibond is a measurement that gauges the color of a substance, in this case, beer. The numbers here will range from light pale lagers that will have a measure of 2°L to imperial stout that has a measure of 70°L. For malts, the range is much greater, as a light crystal of caramel malt will be 20°L, a very dark chocolate malt might be as high as 450, and a black roasted barley malt 500°L.

The grain you use will have to be milled or crushed. If you purchase an ingredient kit, it is likely the grain they included will be crushed. You can purchase crushed grain from a home-brew shop or from an online retailer, but they might not always have the type of malted grain you are looking for that has been crushed. The issue many home brewers have with buying pre-crushed grain is that it is not as fresh. You might liken using pre-crushed grain to buying coffee that has already been ground.

If you get grain that has not been crushed, you might be wondering how to crush it. Grain is hard. The easiest way to go about this is to use your home grain mill. You do not have a home grain mill? Once you become serious about home brewing, it will probably be worth your investment. Before that, however, several options are available to you.

The first thing you can try is to ask the local home-brew retailer that you bought your grain from if they can mill it for you. If you choose this option, make sure you have the grain milled within a couple of days of your brewing day. As soon as the grain is milled, seal it up in an airtight container such as a zip-close bag or some glass jars.

If your local retailer does not have the ability to mill your grain, given that you are not involved in all-grain brewing and the amount of grain that you have to mill is relatively small, you can consider doing it yourself. Actually, there is much to be learned in this task-based experience.

Again, grain is hard. The best way to crush grain without the use of a grain mill is to place a small amount of grain (¾ cup to 1 cup) in a quart freezer bag. Place that quart freezer bag inside of a second quart freezer bag. Make sure both bags are sealed and that most of the air has been squeezed out of them. Use a rolling pin to roll and pound the grain. It is hard work. Your goal is to crush the grain until about 85 percent of the grain has been cracked open. Continue this process until you have crushed all of your grain.

Another method you can try that is much easier but often frowned upon by home brewers is to run the grain through a blender. To do this, pout 1 cup of grain into a blender and use the pulse setting. Pulse the grain three to six times, shaking the blend vessel every two pulses. Then run the blender on the lowest speed for about three seconds. Repeat this process, a cup at a time, until the grain is ground. Note that the directions do not read, "until the grain is crushed." The blender does not crush grain. Blenders grind grain. The difference is that a blender will reduce your grain to flour unless you are careful. Also, blenders rip the hulls away from the interior of the grain and reduce the straining ability of the hull. Again, this is not as big of an issue for the brews that use only a pound or two of grain, but when the quantities increase, the manner of milling does matter.

Brew Note: Though grain mills were not among the list of necessary equipment described in Chapter 4, you might find that they are necessary depending your ability to obtain crushed grain. Grains mills are devices that grind or crush grain, as opposed to devices such as food processors or blenders that chop things. The job of the mill for brewing is to crush the kernel of the grain and leave the hull intact. For grain mills built specifically for home brewers, you can look into Schmidling's MaltMill® (http://schmidling.com/maltmill.htm). This is an excellent type of grain mill built specifically for home brewers. The price ranges between $100 and $150.

- 1 oz. Cascade **or** Willamette hops (60-minute boil)
- ½ oz. Cascade **or** Willamette hops (30-minute boil)
- ½ oz. Cascade **or** Willamette hops (ten-minute boil)
- ½–1 oz. Cascade **or** Willamette hops (dry hop)

If you are brewing from an ingredient kit, the hops offered out of the box might differ from time to time dependent on availability. If you are using an ingredient kit, the hops probably will be in pellet form.

Note that there are time designations listed with the hops. This is known as a hop schedule. The hops added at different times will contribute varying characteristics to the beer.

Hops contribute a variety of characteristics to beer. They give beer a bitterness that offsets the sweetness of the malted barley. Without this balance, beer is another drink in its sweetness. Remember, hops were not used early in beer's history. If you go back to the beer recipes seen in Chapter 1, you will see they are hopless. The beer in this pale ale recipe is mildly hopped, yet the balance offered by the hops in this recipe, and the fact that they are employed to add bitterness, flavor, and aroma, give the beer a good balance.

Hop bitterness is the result of alpha acid in the hop flower. Hops added early in the wort boil go through a breaking down of the acid that adds a certain amount of bitterness to the beer. During the boil, the acid is isomerized and becomes iso-alpha acid. Isomerization is the chemical process whereby a molecule is altered into another molecule with the same atoms. The atoms of this new molecule, however, have been rearranged. This rearrangement of alpha-acid to iso-alpha acid causes the acid to be even bitterer than it started out. Iso-alpha acid is dissolved into the wort and bitters the final beer.

You will remember from Chapter 3 that international bittering units (IBU) measure hop bitterness in beer. One IBU equals about 1 milligram of iso-alpha acid per 1 liter of beer. The IBU range of the Cascade or Willamette hops used in this American pale ale range from four to six on the IBU scale. The final brew will have an IBU in the mid-30s.

Bittering hops do not contribute aroma or flavor beyond bitterness to a beer, yet you will note that hops are quite aromatic and do have a definite flavor. Adding the hops at different times of the wort boil brings out these characteristics.

Because the oils that contribute to flavor and aroma are boiled away in 20 to 30 minutes, you add hops late in the boil or after the boil is complete. Some beer recipes will even instruct you to add aroma hops after a primary fermentation of a week. When hops are added late in the boil or after the boil, they add to the final flavor, aroma, and body of the beer.

Brew Note: Dry hopping is the practice of adding hops to a brew after the boil is complete or even well into the fermentation period. As you will be employing a secondary fermentation technique in this American pale ale, the dry hops will be added at this time. The secondary fermentation will take place about one week after the primary fermentation.

- Wyeast 1056 American ale yeast **or** White Labs WLP American Ale Yeast Blend

You will recall from the Chapter 3 description of yeast that you will use different types and strains of yeast depending on the style of beer. Remember that two basic types of yeast are used in brewing: ale yeast and lager yeast. However, many different varieties of yeast fall into each of these categories. The choice of yeast here will become a matter of preference for you over time. The Wyeast 1056 American ale yeast is a dry yeast that, according to the lab that sells this product (Wyeast Laboratories, **www.wyeastlab.com**) offers "very clean, crisp flavor characteristics." This yeast will perform well if fermented between 60 and 66 degrees.

White Labs WLP American Ale Yeast Blend is liquid yeast. Liquid yeast is simply poured into cooked wort to begin fermentation. White Labs (**www.whitelabs.com**) claims that this yeast is "clean and neutral... versatile usage... (and) creates complexity to the finished beer." This yeast will perform well if fermented between 68 and 72 degrees.

In the end, the yeast you choose now is not that important. Either one of the yeasts mentioned will do a good job for you. Perhaps it is important for you to consider the suggested optimum fermentation temperatures as you make your decision. If you are able to ferment your beer at the lower temperatures, you can choose the dry yeast. If you are in a situation where warmer temperatures are more likely, you can choose the liquid yeast. Of course, availability might make the decision for you. Also, if you are brewing a prepackaged kit, they will include yeast, and it will probably be dry.

- Priming sugar

Priming sugar is added to the beer right before you bottle it. The priming sugar will give the yeast that remains active in your brew the added fuel to carbonate your beer. The best way to add priming sugar to your beer is to add it to the bottling bucket before you transfer the wort from the fermenter.

There are a variety of priming sugars to choose from. If you are preparing from a prepackaged ingredient kit, you will probably get corn sugar. You also can choose to go with white sugar or even dry malt extract.

No matter what you use, you will need to dissolve it in boiling water before adding it to your bottling bucket. Bring 2 cups of water to a boil in a medium saucepan. Add ¾ cup corn sugar (⅔ cup of white sugar, or 1 ¼ cup dry malt extract) to the boiling water and boil for five minutes. Remove the saucepan from the heat and allow it to cool to 110 degrees before adding it to the bottling bucket.

Your choice of priming sugar will play no role in the flavor of your beer.

Steeping the Grains

Brew Note: Always read a recipe all the way through before brewing. Be sure that you know and understand each of the steps involved in the process before you begin.

Uncrushed wheat grains

You are now ready to brew. The first step is to heat a big pot of water on your stove. This pot will need to accommodate at least 3 gallons of water. For this particular recipe, heat 2 ½ gallons of water. You will not boil the water but get it to 150 to 165 degrees. Have your thermometer handy because you will need to hold it at this temperature for 20 to 30 minutes.

Pour the crushed grains into a steeping bag and tie a loose knot at the top of the bag. When the water reaches 150 degrees, gently lower the grain-filled steeping bag into the brew pot of hot water. Steep the grains for 20 to 30 minutes. Be sure to keep the temperature in the 150 to 165 degree range. If the water gets to 170 degrees, tannins will leach from the grains into your wort. Tannins are acids that have a bitter flavor. Water too hot will release the tannic acid from the grain.

After 20 to 30 minutes, remove the steeped grain bag from the water. Do not squeeze the bag, but allow it to drain out into the wort.

For extract brewing, steeping the specialty grains adds flavor and color to your brew. If you were brewing a dark beer such as porter or stout, you would notice that the wort is nearly black at this stage. For the American pale ale you are brewing, the color of the wort now will depend on whether you chose to steep the dark crystal malt or the caramel malt. The dark malt will result in darker wort.

The steeped grain can be discarded. You can throw it away or put it in your home compost pile.

Adding the Malt Extract

Now that the specialty grain has been steeped, it is time to add the fermentables, that is, the malt extract. The first step in doing this is to bring the wort to a boil. Raise the heat on your brew pot, and allow it to boil.

As soon as the wort starts to boil, remove the wort from the heat. Add half of the malt extract (LME or DME). The malt extracts will behave differently depending on the type you add. Whether you choose LME or DME, stir them in well.

If you are using LME, it helps to let the canister of LME sit in a sink full of hot water before you open it to add it to your pot. LME is a thick honey-like substance. Warming it up in a hot water bath will make it easier to pour.

If you are using LME, you need to be sure to stir from the bottom of the pot, as the LME will sink immediately to the bottom. Keep the LME from sitting on the bottom of the pot.

If you are using DME, you will notice that it clots thickly on the surface of the wort when you add it to the pot. Stirring the wort well will help to dissolve the DME.

Stir until the malt extract is well dispersed into the wort before you return the pot to the heat. When you return the pot to the heat, bring it to a boil.

Brew Note: As you learn and read more about brewing beer, you will find that the process that began simply and quite naturally can be, on the other hand, scientific. You will, at times, feel as if you are taking a chemistry class when you start to read about the various processes and techniques involved in brewing. This is mentioned here because there are various theories about the best time to add malt extract. Many recipes call for you to add all of the malt extract at the beginning of the boil, and there is no mention of taking the pot off the heat before adding the extract. But many extract brewers do not believe the malt extract should be boiled at all. The argument against boiling the malt extract is that by waiting until the boil is complete to add the malt extract, the resulting beer will be lighter in color, have a higher level of hop bitterness, and minimize the carmelization of the malt extract sugars, which will result in more appropriate malt flavors.

Adding Hops

Once the wort has returned to a good rolling boil, add 1 ounce of the hops. These hops are the bittering hops. Most, if not all, beer recipes you come across will include a hop schedule. The hop schedule for this brew is:

- 1 oz. Cascade **or** Willamette hops (60-minute boil)
- ½ oz. Cascade **or** Willamette hops (30-minute boil)

- ½ oz. Cascade **or** Willamette hops (ten-minute boil)
- ½–1 oz. Cascade **or** Willamette hops (dry hop)

Hops in pellet form. Photo courtesy of www.KirksBrew.com

This hops schedule informs you that the total time you will boil the wort is 60 minutes. You add one ounce of hops at the start of the boil; add ½ ounce of hops 30 minutes into the boil; ½ ounce of hops 40 minutes into the boil. The final hop addition will come a week or so into fermentation.

The first hops you add to this brew are the bittering hops. You will remember that hops added early in the wort boil go through a breakdown of the acid that adds a certain amount of bitterness to the beer. During the boil, the acid is isomerized and becomes iso-alpha acid. Iso-alpha acid is even bitterer than alpha acid. This is the reason a hop will have a lower IBU before it is boiled than the IBU of the final brew. Iso-alpha acid is dissolved into the wort and bitters the final beer.

The second hop addition is the flavoring hop. Because the oils that contribute to flavor and aroma are boiled away in 20 to 30 minutes, you add hops late in the boil or after the boil is complete. When hops are added late in the boil or after the boil, they add to the final flavor, aroma, and body of the beer. The timing of when you add hops will determine the resulting flavor. In this case, these flavoring hops are added 30 minutes into the boil, which will reduce their flavor considerably.

Many beer recipes will call for a variety of hop types to be used. You may employ one variety of hop as a bittering hop, another variety as a flavoring hop, and a third or a fourth variety as additional flavoring and/or aroma hops.

The third hop addition in this recipe will add to the flavor and the aroma of the beer. This will be indicated on the recipe as the aroma hop. As this hop addition is boiled for only ten minutes, it will retain much of the oil that contributes to the flavor and aroma of the final beer.

The dry hop addition will be discussed further on in this chapter.

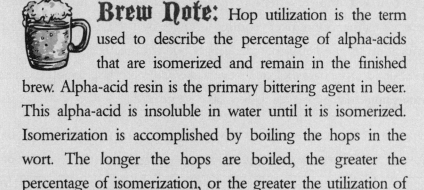 **Brew Note:** Hop utilization is the term used to describe the percentage of alpha-acids that are isomerized and remain in the finished brew. Alpha-acid resin is the primary bittering agent in beer. This alpha-acid is insoluble in water until it is isomerized. Isomerization is accomplished by boiling the hops in the wort. The longer the hops are boiled, the greater the percentage of isomerization, or the greater the utilization of the hop, and the more bitter the brew.

Late Extract Addition

You should add the remaining malt extract 40 minutes into the boil. Again, if you are using LME, it helps to let the canister of LME sit in a sink full of hot water before you open it to add it to your pot.

Before adding the extract, remove the pot from the heat. Add the extract, and stir it well to keep it off the bottom of the pot or to help dissolve it. As soon as the extract is well stirred into your wort, return the wort to the heat, and boil as you continue to add the hops.

As you gain experience in brewing, you will note how the color of the wort changes as it is boiled. The late addition of the malt extract in this recipe is to help the beer achieve its proper pale amber color.

Complete Boil and Cool

The boil is complete after 60 minutes for this particular American pale ale recipe. Some beer requires a longer boil to ensure proper hop utilization. A good example of a longer boil is India pale ale or imperial pale ale (double pale ale) that have extremely high hop profiles. These brews might be boiled for as long as 75 minutes.

Once the boil is complete, remove the pot from the heat. The goal now is to chill the wort as quickly as possible. The quicker the wort is chilled, the less chance there is that it will be contaminated by unwanted bacteria. Chilling the wort can be accomplished in a number of different ways. The easiest way to begin the cool is to set the pot of hot wort in a sink full of cold water. Stirring the wort helps to cool it at this point. The temperature of the boiling wort is just over 200 degrees, and you will need to cool it to about 70 degrees to pitch the yeast. If you are chilling your wort in a sink filled with ice, it may take an hour or two to get it down to the target temperature. If your cooking/cooling environment is clean, you should not have any worries about contamination. The yeast you use will determine the precise target temperature. Check the yeast package and follow the directions for optimum pitching temperature.

While the wort is beginning to cool, you should ensure your fermenter, siphon, hose, thermometer, and hydrometer have been properly cleaned and sanitized.

The recipe you are making is for 5 gallons of beer. You began your steeping and boiling stages with 2 ½ gallons of water. Once your wort cools to about 160 degrees, you can expedite the cooling of the wort by transferring the hot wort to your fermenter and adding 1 ½ gallons of water that is 65 to 70 degrees. After you add the cold water, check the temperature of the wort. You will need to continue chilling it. Add some ice to that sink bath and place your fermenter in the ice water. If it is winter and you have snow on the ground, a snow bank is perfect for quickly chilling your hot wort.

The reason you want to chill the wort as quickly as possible is to reduce the chance that some bad bacteria might enter your warm wort and contaminate it. To reduce the chance of this happening, you need to chill the wort as quickly as possible, pitch the yeast, and cover the fermenter.

Brew Note: Another piece of equipment that is not absolutely necessary but can come in handy at this time is a wort chiller. A wort chiller is a device used to cool boiling wort to yeast pitching temperatures quickly. The two most popular types of wort chillers are the immersion chiller and the counter-flow chiller. The immersion chiller is made from of a coil of copper tubing submerged in the hot wort. Cold water runs through the copper tubing and expedites the cooling of the wort. A counter-flow chiller is made from of copper tubing that runs inside of a larger diameter plastic tube. Cold water runs through the plastic tubing in one direction, and the wort flows through the copper tubing in the other direction.

A wort chiller is used to cool wort quickly for several reasons. You do not need to wait so long to get your wort to the desired yeast pitching temperature, and

Immersion chiller. Photo courtesy of www.KirksBrew.com

you lower the risk of wort contamination. A basic wort chiller can be purchased from local home-brew stores or online retailers for about $60.

Measure the OG (Original Gravity)

As your wort cools to near 70 degrees and before you pitch the yeast, measure the gravity of the beer. Follow the directions for using the hydrometer from Chapter 4. The original gravity of this beer should be between 1.051 and 1.055. As you take the hydrometer reading, do not forget to account for temperature variations in your beer. Remember that the hydrometer is calibrated to give a normal reading at 59 degrees.

Because you started to brew a 5-gallon batch of beer, and you began with 2 ½ gallons of water and added 1 ½ gallons to cool, your gravity probably will read a little high. To bring the gravity to the range you are targeting, add cool water to bring your beer to about 4 ½ gallons. Take another hydrometer reading. If your gravity is still a little high, add another quart of cool water and read the hydrometer again. You should be close to your target number by now. If you are still a little off, add water to exactly 5 gallons and take a reading.

If you have gotten to the point of your first hydrometer reading and your gravity is too low, you have several options available to you that are either simple, or not as simple as adding water (how you adjusted for a gravity that was too high.) You can do nothing and just go with it. The resulting beer will not be as high in alcohol content as it might have been if your gravity was in the desired range. If you want to bring your gravity up a bit, you could consider boiling a little more extract if you have it for about 15 minutes in a quart of water. Cool the mixture to the temperature of the wort in the fermenter, and stir it in a little at a time, taking hydrometer readings as you do this.

Because your hydrometer readings are more likely to be high rather than low as you take your readings, you probably will not have to face this last scenario. Brewing with malt extract and following the directions carefully should be fairly foolproof.

Pitching the Yeast

Pitching the yeast is merely the brewing term for adding yeast to the wort. Before this is done, it is critical that the wort is the correct temperature, as described in the last section. If the wort is too warm, it could kill the yeast. If the wort is too cool, the yeast will remain dormant or get off to a slow start. Pitching yeast into a cool environment is preferable to pitching it into a too hot environment. If your wort is too cool when you pitch your yeast, just make sure that as you begin the fermentation process, your fermenter is in a place at the temperature that is friendly to the specific yeast you are using. Every yeast strain is different, so it is vital that you pay close attention to the recipe and the optimum temperatures on the yeast packets.

Yeast thrives on sugars, moisture, and oxygen. You provide the sugars and liquid by offering your wort to the yeast. To provide oxygen, you need to aerate the wort after you pitch the yeast. Stirring the wort after the yeast has been added does the task of aerating the wort. Stir the wort well.

As you read more about brewing, you will come across the term "yeast pitching rate." A yeast pitching rate is the amount of yeast added to the cooled wort. These rates are noted as millions of yeast cells per millimeter of wort. The yeast pitching rate will be explored more fully as you progress from beginning brewing to intermediate and advanced brewing.

Fermentation

The grain is steeped. The malt extract and hops are cooked. The yeast is pitched and aerated. Now comes the hard part. Patience.

Place the cover on your beer, and put the airlock in place. Every beer will have a slightly different temperature best for fermentation. This American pale ale is best fermented between 64 and 72 degrees. Be sure the fermenter is in a relatively dark place out of direct sunlight. If the fermenter is placed in an area that experiences direct sunlight, it will get too warm, and the temperature fluctuation will be too great.

Because you will be putting this brew through a secondary fermentation, you will want to place this primary fermenter in a location where you will not be required to move it to transfer the brew from the primary to the secondary fermenter. If you can place this primary fermenter on a table or bench to allow for easy siphoning, all the better. If you move the primary fermenter just before transferring from primary to secondary, you risk kicking up the yeast that will gather at the bottom of the fermenter, and you do not want them accidentally transferred to the secondary container.

Within the first 12 hours, you will start to notice fermentation. Fermentation will be seen as carbon dioxide escapes from the airlock. Over the first 24 hours, you will see an increase in activity. The activity will increase over the period of about 48 hours and then begin to slow over the period of 48 hours. After about four or five days, you will see that little to no carbon dioxide is escaping from the fermenter.

After a week in this primary fermentation stage, you will be ready to transfer your brew to a secondary fermenter.

Secondary Fermentation and Dry Hopping

Most brews do not need to be transferred to a secondary fermentation vessel, and most home brewers will tell you they do not engage in secondary fermentation. The reason they will give you is that whenever you open your fermenter, your brew is susceptible to contamination. Also, one of the primary reasons for secondary fermentation is to improve beer clarity, and most home brewers are just not that concerned about beer that is mildly cloudy. They think that the prospect of contamination is too great of a trade-off.

Other reasons that you might consider secondary fermentation are a late hop addition or to add a particular flavoring agent. Also, if you plan to ferment a beer for a longer period than a couple of weeks, you might consider secondary fermentation to get the beer off the yeast that has dropped to the bottom of the primary fermenter. If the beer sits on that yeast for an extended period (say, four weeks), it may develop an off flavor from the yeast.

The fact is, if you are careful about cleaning and sanitizing your equipment, you will, more than likely, not experience contamination. Again, before you open your primary fermenter and begin the transfer into a secondary fermenter, be sure that your equipment is clean.

The secondary fermentation stage is being described here for several reasons. This American ale recipe calls for a dry-hop procedure. Also, the description of the process of secondary fermentation, while relatively simple, is edifying.

The secondary fermenter can be another fermentation bucket or a carboy (glass or plastic). The secondary fermenter also should have a lid or cap that allows for an airlock.

After you have cleaned and sanitized your secondary fermenter, siphon, and transfer hose, you can remove the lid of the primary fermenter. Take care to keep things that may fall into your brew well clear. Make sure anything that comes into contact with your brew is clean and sanitary.

Lower the siphon into the brew in the fermenter, being careful not to draw from the bottom of the bucket. There will be a thick layer of yeast at the bottom of the fermenter. Lower the hose to the very bottom of the secondary fermenter. Your task is to siphon the beer out of the primary fermenter and into the secondary fermenter leaving the sludge behind and not splashing the beer into the secondary fermenter during the transfer. As the secondary fermenter begins to fill, keep the hose beneath the surface of the incoming beer.

As the secondary fermenter is about half filled, gently add the ½ to 1 oz. of Cascade **or** Willamette hops. Adding the hops at this point is known as dry hopping. These are strictly aromatic hops.

As you get to the bottom of the beer in the primary fermenter, you can tip the fermenter gently to ease the transfer of the last of the beer, being careful not to get the sludge on the bottom.

Plug or cap the secondary fermenter, and insert a clean airlock. If you only have one airlock, you will need to clean and sanitize the airlock that was in place on the primary fermenter for use on the secondary fermenter.

As previously mentioned, this American pale ale is best fermented in the secondary fermenter between 64 and 72 degrees. Be sure the secondary fermenter is in a relatively dark place out of direct sunlight. Although you were careful to avoid transferring the yeast on the bottom of the primary fermenter, yeast suspended in the brew still was transferred to the secondary fermenter. If the secondary fermenter is placed in sunlight, the brew will suffer from the regular temperature fluctuation of the day. The temperature needs to be relatively constant.

You might have thought fermentation had ended, but after you transfer to the secondary fermenter you might notice new activity. The airlock might come to life again. This is normal.

The brew will remain in the secondary fermenter for two weeks. If you are patient, you can leave the beer in a secondary fermentation for two months. The effect this longer secondary fermentation will have is that the beer will be clearer than the beer bottled after two weeks.

Priming and Bottling

The beer has been fermented, and what sits in your secondary fermenter at this point is alcohol. After a two-week (or longer) secondary fermentation, you can gather your clean bottle and caps and clean and sterilize your hydrometer, thermometer, siphon, hose, and bottling wand. If you used a carboy as a secondary fermenter, you also might need a tool to draw some of the beer out of the carboy before you transfer it into the bottling bucket. A good tool for this is an old-fashioned turkey baster.

Before you transfer your beer from the secondary fermenter to the bottling bucket, you have a couple of tasks to attend to. The first task is to take a gravity reading. This particular reading will result in a number that will be your final gravity (FG). Before you take a hydrometer reading, use the cleaned and sanitized thermometer to note the temperature of the beer. You might have a fermometer on the side of your secondary fermenter that will give you a good indication of the beer's temperature, but a thermometer reading here will be a little more accurate. If you used a bucket as a secondary fermenter, you can simply lower the cleaned and sanitized hydrometer into the beer and take that reading. If you used a carboy, you can use the cleaned and sanitized turkey baster to draw some of the beer out of the carboy and transfer it into a tall and narrow receptacle. The receptacle will have to be tall enough to accommodate the floating hydrometer. The receptacle should be narrow so you do not have to draw out too much beer. Take the hydrometer reading, and remember to take the temperature of the beer into account when you calculate your FG. The FG of this brew should be in the range of 1.012 to 1.015. If your reading falls out of this range slightly, do not worry about it. If your number is wildly out of this range, your hydrometer is not working properly, or you went wrong somewhere in the brewing process. As was mentioned earlier, brewing with malt extract and following the directions carefully is pretty foolproof. If you are somewhere in the FG range and your beer does not smell or look bad, go ahead with your bottling.

Using the original gravity (OG) number and the final gravity (FG) number, you can now calculate the ABV (alcohol by volume).

(OG – FG) x 131 = ABV%

Let us assume that your OG was 1.051 and your FG is 1.012. If you plug those numbers into the above formula you get:

(1.051 – 1.012) x 131 = 5.1 percent alcohol by volume

Brew Note: Let it be said here that the formula given on the previous page is not an exact measurement, but it does come close enough to the number sought that it is used fairly universally. The multiplier used in this formula (131.25) is known as the "f value" and is not constant. This number might be 129 or 132. This number applies to a correction factor connecting change in gravity with alcoholic strength, and this number can range from 125 to 135. Any more explanation than this can get complicated. If you want to get more specific about your measurement, you might use this table developed by the Laboratory of the Government Chemist in the United Kingdom for alcohol taxation purposes.

Table 1. f values for various beer strengths (HM Revenue and Customs (UK) 2008)

(OG – FG)	% ABV	Factor (f)
Up to 0.0069	Up to 0.8	125
0.0070–0.0104	0.8–1.3	126
0.0105–0.0172	1.3–2.1	127
0.0173–0.0261	2.2–3.3	128
0.0262–0.0360	3.3–4.6	129
0.0361–0.0465	4.6–6.0	130
0.0466–0.0571	6.0–7.5	131
0.0572–0.0679	7.5–9.0	132
0.0680–0.0788	9.0–10.5	133
0.0789–0.0897	10.5–12.0	134
0.0898–0.1007	12.0–13.6	135

In the end, it might be simpler to go with the mid-ground number of 131.

Finally, you are ready to bottle your American pale ale. Heat two cups of water in a medium saucepan to a boil. Add ½ to ¾ cup white granulated table sugar or corn sugar to the boiling water. Stir the sugar in until it has dissolved, and allow it to boil for five minutes.

Remove the sugar water from the heat, and pour it into the cleaned and sanitized bottling bucket. Be sure the spigot on the bucket is closed.

Use the cleaned and sanitized siphon and hose to transfer the beer from the secondary fermenter into the bottling bucket. As you transfer your beer, avoid transferring any sediment that may be on the bottom of the secondary fermenter.

After all the beer has been transferred, remove the hose from the bottling bucket, and if you feel as though you want to stir, do so very gently, though you probably do not need to.

Attach the hose (minus the siphon) to the spigot of the bottling bucket. Attach the other end of the hose to the bottling wand. Place some of your cleaned and sanitized bottles into a large pot, or something that will catch any spilled beer. Put the end of the bottling wand into a bottle and open the spigot of the bottling bucket. When you touch the bottom of the bottle with the end of the bottling wand, a valve will release, and beer will flow from the bottling bucket into the bottle. When the bottle is filled to within an inch of the top, raise the bottling wand. Raising the bottling wand will stop the flow of beer. Repeat this process until all of the beer has been transferred from the bottling bucket. You will have between 46 and 52 bottles of beer from your 5-gallon batch. If you have a small amount of beer remaining in the bottom of your bottling bucket, pour it into a glass, and give it a taste.

The beer will be flat and unconditioned, but it will give you some indication of what you have produced.

Use your capper to place cleaned and sanitized crimp caps on each of the filled bottles. If the bottles have any residual beer on them, use a damp cloth to wipe them off.

Find a cool dark place to put your bottled beer to allow it to bottle condition. There is an old rule of home-brew thumb that goes "1 week to ferment; 2 weeks to secondary ferment; 3 weeks to bottle condition." This does not mean that you cannot give your beer a taste after two weeks. It is better after three weeks, though.

Patience.

Kegging

If and when you decide to store your brew in kegs rather than, or along with, bottles, you will follow these steps:

1. Clean and sanitize the keg. Your keg will be made of stainless steel, so make sure your cleaning agent is safe to use on stainless steel.

2. Use the gas to pressurize the tank to make sure there are no leaks in the system. After you pressurize the tank, you can put

a little soapy water around all of the fittings. If there is a leak, you will see bubbles form.

3. Siphon your beer from your fermenter (primary or secondary, depending on the recipe) into the keg. As you siphon the beer, be careful not to aerate the beer by splashing it. You can do this by keeping your siphon hose below the surface of the incoming beer.

4. After you have filled the keg, put the lid on it.

5. Pressurize the tank with CO_2. To do this, attach the hose from the CO_2 tank to the CO_2 intake valve on the keg. Open the valve to the CO_2 tank and add the appropriate amount of CO_2. Different beers and tastes will require varying levels of CO_2. To see a good calculator that will help you achieve a good suggested amount of pressure for your brew, check out the carbonation calculator at The Beer Recipator (**http://hbd. org/cgi-bin/recipator/recipator/carbonation.html**).

6. Force any remaining air out of the keg. You will do this by releasing the air in the keg's headspace and replacing it with CO_2.

7. After the keg has been pressurized, you can store it in a refrigerator to carbonate.

Brew note: Most home brewers force carbonate kegged beer. They do not use a primer on their beer before putting it into kegs; rather, they use CO_2 and refrigeration over a couple of days to carbonate the brew. The upside to kegging and force pressuring the beer with CO_2 is that you can enjoy your immediately and not have to wait for the beer to carbonate.

What Might Go Wrong Along the Way

It has been stated on several occasions that if you are brewing from a boxed kit, or if you have a good and clear recipe and you read and follow the directions closely, you will face few problems along the way. That is not to say that problems cannot arise. It just means brewing is a forgiving process.

Clean and sanitary

You will note the number of times the words "cleaned and sanitized" appeared in the directions above. From this you can see the No. 1 issue that might arise to spoil your investment in ingredients and waste the time you spend brewing your beer is contamination brought about by unclean equipment. Do not let this happen to you.

Tannins

During the steeping stage, you need to be careful about the temperatures of your water. If your water gets too hot, unwanted tannins will leach into your wort. Tannins are acids that have a bitter flavor. Water that is too hot will release the tannic acid from the grain. If, during your steeping stage, you notice the water has risen, or is rising, to temperatures above 168 degrees, remove the wort from the heat for a few moments and reduce the heat on the burner. Check the temperature of the wort to see it down past 160 degrees before returning the wort to the heat.

Likewise, after you are done with the steeping stage and you remove your steeped grains in the steeping bag from the wort, do not squeeze the bag. This action, again, will squeeze unwanted tannins into your wort. Allow the wort to simply drain from the steeping bag.

Boil-over

 As you increase the heat under your wort to a boil after you have added the malt extract, beware of boil-over. The malt solution you have added to the heat is extremely susceptible to producing a bubbly boil-over. Keep an eye on it. If you see that the wort is about to boil over, remove the pot from the heat momentarily, and allow the brew to stabilize.

Excessive fermentation

Early in the fermentation process, you might notice the beer seems to be excessively active. Excessive fermentation might cause the beer to bubble up into the airlock. You can put this activity in check for the day or two of excessive fermentation by attaching a blow-off tube to the fermenter. A blow-off tube is simply a tube that runs from the opening in the top of the fermenter out of the vessel and into a jar that has a little sanitizing solution in it. It acts like an extended airlock. You still want gas to escape the fermenter while not allowing anything from the outside into the fermenter. A blow-off hose will accomplish this.

Brew note: If you experience an excessively active fermentation that blows the lid off your fermenter, all is not lost. If you have handled your brewing in a sanitary manner and you catch your exploding brew before the active fermentation has ceased, clean your fermenter lid with a sanitary solution and place it back on the fermenter with a blow-off hose in place. Keep a close eye on the fermenter to make sure the blow-off hose does not get clogged. Once the excessive fermentation settles down, you can put the airlock back on the fermenter.

Contamination during fermentation

If you find that your beer develops an off smell during the fermentation process, such as an extremely sour smell, a rotten egg smell, or a dirty diaper smell, you did something wrong. For contamination issues, there is no fix other than to throw it out, clean your equipment more thoroughly, and start again.

Stuck fermentation

If you go through the steeping, boiling, and yeast pitching stages and your beer does not ferment, you might have pitched your yeast at a temperature that was too high, thus killing the yeast. If you believe this to be the case, you can try to pitch more yeast. By this time, the wort probably will be at a proper temperature. Pitch more yeast, replace the fermenter and airlock, and cross your fingers.

On the other hand, if you think that the wort might have been too cool when you pitched your yeast, you might just have to wait it out. The yeast might be sluggish. Get your fermenting beer to a location that is in the optimum fermenting temperature, and you might see activity. If not, try re-pitching the yeast.

Over carbonation

Beer that has been bottled before fermentation has completed runs the risk of being overly carbonated and might cause bottles to explode. Do not let this happen to you. Exploding bottles are not only messy, but also dangerous as well. If you experience a bursting bottle or bottles, you might be able to save the rest of your batch by placing the bottles in closed containers and cooling or refrigerating them.

Beer that has been contaminated in some manner also might produce excessive carbonation. You will experience either burst bottles that have an overly yeasty smell, or you will notice the smell as you open the beer. Unfortunately, there is nothing you can do to salvage the beer at this point.

Mold

If, during the fermentation stage or the bottle conditioning stage, you become aware of a white film on the surface of your beer, you can be sure an airborne mold has attacked your brew. If you notice this during the primary fermenting stage, you might be able to transfer the beer by siphoning it off from below the mold. Even if you notice mold in the secondary fermenter or even in your bottled beer, you do not need to throw the beer away. The mold will not harm you; it is just unpleasant to look at.

Chill haze

If you read home-brew message boards online you might be aware that this is probably one of biggest issues home brewers face. The problem of hazy or unclear beer plagues home brewers. You might notice that your beer is clear at room temperature, but when it is chilled, it develops a haze. Proteins and tannins that clump together when beer is chilled cause this haze. In most cases, this haze has no effect at all on the taste of the beer.

Commercial brewers combat this chill haze by chilling the beer and then running it through a fine filter. You, as a beginning home brewer, probably will not be able to accomplish this. The best thing you can do to fight chill haze is to boil the beer as hard as possible during the boiling stage and then to chill it as quickly as possible after the boil is complete. These processes of a good hard rolling boil and then a quick chill (called a cold break) will eliminate these protein clumps or cause them to drop to the bottom of the chilled wort.

Your First Taste

You have been so patient. You spent four or five hours preparing your ingredients, cleaning your equipment, steeping your grains, boiling and cooling your wort, pitching your yeast, and setting your beer to ferment. You waited a week to transfer your beer into the secondary fermenter. You patiently waited two weeks while your beer completed secondary fermentation before you bottled your beer. Now, you have waited two or three weeks to allow your beer time to bottle condition and carbonate. Finally, it is time to reward yourself and taste the fruits of your labor and patience.

Take a bottle or two of your home brew and put them in the refrigerator for a couple of hours to chill. Ideally, you should serve American pale ale at 40 degrees. You might be used to drinking commercial beer from bottles, but it is best to pour your homebrew into a glass. You will notice a little yeast that has formed at the bottom of the bottle as the beer has conditioned. Leave this yeast behind as you pour the beer into the glass. You do not have to pour the beer short out of the bottle, just avoid swishing the beer around in the bottle as you pour.

The American pale ale you have brewed will offer a good balance of malt and hop character, with neither character giving over too much to the other. The beer will not be overly bitter, nor will it be sweet. American pale ale is a great beer to enjoy with a variety of foods, as it will not overpower the palate and is clean in taste.

Chapter 6:
Extract Recipes

The recipes included are basic recipes that employ malt extract and specialty grains. All of the recipes included here are for basic beer styles and can be made using only the essential ingredients described in Chapter 3 and the equipment described in Chapter 4.

You will rarely, if ever, come across a recipe that is as fully described as that for American pale ale in the previous chapter. The recipes you discover online, in home-brew books, and in magazines will be much  briefer. Often, you will not get much more than a list of ingredients, a hop schedule, and the OG and FG numbers. The assumption is that you know the rest.

The recipes offered in this chapter will be presented in several different formats that will range from less descriptive than the American ale recipe presented in Chapter 5 yet still fully described, to a recipe that will offer the bare bones of a brew.

American Amber Ale

5 gallons, extract with grains; OG = 1.050; FG = 1.01; IBUs = 16

Ingredients:

Fermentables:

5 lbs. Munton's Extra-Light DME

Specialty Malts:

½ lb. crystal malt (20°L)

½ lb. crystal malt (40°L)

½ lb. carapils malt

½ lb. Munich malt

½ lb. biscuit malt

½ lb. chocolate malt

Hops:

⅔ oz. Willamette pellet hops (4.5% alpha acid)

⅓ oz. Styrian Goldings pellet hops (4% alpha acid)

½ oz. Styrian Goldings pellet hops (4% alpha acid)

Adjunct:

1 tsp. Irish moss

Yeast:

Wyeast 1056 American Ale Yeast

Primer

⅔ cup corn sugar

Directions:

1. Place ½ lb. crystal malt (20L), ½ lb. crystal malt (40L), ½ lb. carapils malt, ½ lb. Munich malt, ½ lb. biscuit malt, ½ lb. chocolate malt (specialty grains) in a steeping bag.

2. Steep specialty grains in 3 gallons of water at 154 degrees F for 45 minutes.

3. Remove grains from steeping water and allow to drain into wort without squeezing bag.

4. Bring wort to boil.

5. Remove wort from heat.

6. Add DME to wort, and stir well.

7. Return wort to heat.

8. Add ⅔ oz. Willamette pellet hops.

9. Boil for 60 minutes.

10. Add Irish moss.

11. Boil ten minutes.

12. Add ½ oz. Styrian Goldings pellet hops.

13. Boil 20 minutes.

14. Remove from heat.

15. Add remaining Styrian Goldings pellet hops.

16. Cool to 80 degrees.

17. Transfer to fermenting vessel.

18. Add cool 60- to 70-degree water to bring volume to 5 gallons.

19. When temperature reaches 70 degrees, pitch yeast and stir well.

20. Cap fermenting vessel and place airlock.

21. Ferment at 64 to 68 degrees seven to ten days.

22. Transfer to a secondary fermenter and allow to ferment at 64 to 68 degrees for two weeks.

23. Heat 2 cups of water to rolling boil in a medium saucepan.

24. Add ⅔ cup priming sugar, and stir well.

25. Cook sugar water for five minutes.

26. Pour sugar water into bottling bucket.

27. Transfer beer from secondary fermenter into bottling bucket.

28. Transfer beer from bottling bucket into bottles, and cap bottles.

29. Allow beer to bottle condition for a minimum of two weeks, though two months is preferred for best results.

Light American Ale

Here is a recipe that requires only a malt extract. No grain steeping is required, which makes this the simplest recipe in the book. This is a great beer for a hot summer day.

5 gallons; OG = 1.040; FG = 1.010; IBU = 20; ABV = 3.8%

Ingredients:

Fermentables:

6 lbs. Briess Pilsen dry malt extract DME

Hops:

1 oz. Hallertau hops (55 minutes) (4.5% alpha acids)

1 oz. Hallertau hops (5 minutess) (4.5% alpha acids)

Yeast:

Wyeast 1187 (Ringwood Ale) yeast

Primer:

¾ cup corn sugar (for priming)

Directions:

1. Bring 3 gallons of water to boil in a brew pot.

2. Add DME to water and stir well.

3. Return wort to heat.

4. Add 1 oz. Hallertau pellet hops.

5. Boil 60 minutes.

6. Add remaining Hallertau pellet hops and boil five additional minutes.

7. Cool to 80 degrees.

8. Transfer to fermenting vessel.

9. Add cool 60- to 70-degree water to bring volume to 5 gallons.

10. When temperature reaches 70 degrees, pitch yeast, and stir well.

11. Cap fermenting vessel, and place airlock.

12. Ferment at 64 to 68 degrees seven to ten days.

13. Transfer to a secondary fermenter, and allow to ferment at 64 to 68 degrees for two weeks.

14. Heat 2 cups of water to rolling boil in a medium saucepan.

15. Add ¾ cup priming sugar and stir well.

16. Cook sugar water for five minutes.

17. Pour sugar water into bottling bucket.

18. Transfer beer from secondary fermenter into bottling bucket.

19. Transfer beer from bottling bucket into bottles, and cap bottles.

20. Allow beer to bottle condition for a minimum of two weeks, though two months is preferred for best results.

Scottish Strong Ale

This recipe is slightly more abbreviated than the one above. The abbreviation comes in the description of the boil and the hop additions (referred to as the hop schedule.) When a recipe notes the hop schedule, the number of minutes listed describes how long you should boil that particular dose of hops. For example, in this recipe for Scottish strong ale, the total boil time is 60 minutes. The bittering hops will be boiled for 60 minutes, so add them right at the beginning of the boil. The second hop addition (flavoring hops) comes with 20 minutes remaining on the boil, so 40 minutes after you added the first hops and began boiling. The third addition (flavoring and aroma hops) is the "finishing hops," which are boiled for ten minutes. So, you would add them after 50 minutes of boiling. The final hop addition is made at the end of the boil and is considered the dry hop. It should be added after the pot is removed from the heat (aroma hop).

5 gallons/19 L, extract with grains; OG = 1.060;
FG = 1.013; IBU = 40; ABV = 6.1%

Ingredients:

Fermentables:

2 ½ lbs. Muntons Light dried malt extract

4 lbs. Alexander's Pale liquid malt extract

Specialty Malts:

2 lbs crystal malt (75°L)

½ oz. chocolate malt

Hops:

1 oz. Challenger hops (60 minutes) (7% alpha acids)

1 oz. Challenger hops (20 minutes) (7% alpha acids)

⅔ oz. East Kent Goldings hops (ten minutes) (5% alpha acids)

1 ¼ oz. East Kent Goldings hops (0 minutes)

Adjuncts:

1 tsp. Irish moss (15 minutes)

Yeast

Wyeast 1968 (London ESB) or White Labs WLP002 (English Ale) yeast

Primer:

¾ cup corn sugar

Directions:

1. In a small pot, heat ¾ gallon of water to 154 degrees.

2. Place specialty grains in a steeping bag.

3. Steep the specialty grains in the ¾ gallon of water for 30 to 45 minutes.

4. Remove specialty grains steeping bag and allow it to drain into smaller pot.

5. Heat 2 ¼ gallons of water in large brew pot to 170 degrees.

6. Add steeped liquid from smaller pot to 2 ¼ gallons in larger pot.

7. Add 2 ½ lbs. Muntons Light dried malt extract to brew pot, and bring to a boil.

8. Add hops and Irish moss following hop schedule in ingredient list.

9. With 15 minutes left in the boil, remove brew pot from heat.

10. Stir in 4 lbs. Alexander's Pale liquid malt extract. Stir well.

11. Return to heat for remainder of time indicated.

12. After 60 minutes, remove from heat, and cool to 80 degrees.

13. Siphon to fermenter.

14. Add cool water to make 5 gallons.

15. When wort reaches 70 degrees, pitch yeast, and stir well.

16. Ferment at 68 to 70 degrees for two weeks.

17. Heat 2 cups of water to rolling boil in a medium saucepan.

18. Add ¾ cup priming sugar, and stir well.

19. Cook sugar water for five minutes.

20. Pour sugar water into bottling bucket.

21. Transfer beer from secondary fermenter into bottling bucket.

22. Transfer beer from bottling bucket into bottles, and cap bottles.

23. Allow beer to bottle condition for a minimum of two weeks, though two months is preferred for best results.

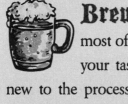 **Brew note:** You can make substitutions for most of the ingredients in any given recipe to suit your taste and/or product availability. If you are new to the process and unsure about any substitution you may need to make, do your homework and look into ingredient suitability. You can do research online at any of the many home-brew websites noted in the resource directory in this book. Better yet, talk to your local home-brew retailer. In most cases, they will be happy to steer you in the right direction.

Porter

5 gallons/19 L, extract w/grains; OG = 1.064; FG = 1.016; IBU = 27; ABV = 6.2%

Ingredients:

Fermentables:

1 lb. Briess Light dried malt extract (DME)

4 ⅔ lbs. Briess Light liquid malt extract (LME) (late addition)

Specialty Malts

2 ⅓ lbs. Bonlander Munich malt

1 ¼ lbs. crystal malt (40°L)

1 ¼ lbs. crystal malt (80°L)

¾ lb. chocolate malt

¼ lb. black malt

Hops:

¼ oz. Chinook hop (90 minutes) (14% alpha acids)

½ oz. Northern Brewer hops (30 minutes) (6% alpha acids)

¾ oz. Northern Brewer hops (0 minutes)

Yeast:

1 pkg. Nottingham Ale Yeast

Primer:

¾ cup corn sugar (for priming)

Directions:

1. Heat 2 gallons of water to 152 degrees in a large brew pot.

2. Place specialty malts in a steeping bag. Steep at 152 degrees.

3. Allow specialty grains to steep at 152 degrees for 60 minutes.

4. Heat 1 gallon of water in a large saucepan to 170 degrees.

5. Remove steeping bag from brew pot.

6. Place steeping bag in a large colander, and allow it to drain into brew pot.

7. Slowly rinse specialty grains with the 1-gallon of 170-degree water in the saucepan. The best way to do this is to place the grain bag in a colander and pour the hot water over it into the brew pot.

8. Add dried malt extract to brew pot, and stir well.

9. Raise heat on brew pot, and bring to a boil.

10. Follow hop schedule for a total boil of 90 minutes.

11. Do not let the wort volume go below 2 ¼ gallons. To do this, keep a kettle of water boiling separately that you may add during the 90-minute boil.

12. With ten minutes remaining in boil, remove brew pot from heat and add LME.

13. Stir well.

14. Return to boil for remainder of 90-minute boil.

15. After 90 minutes, remove from heat, and make final hop addition.

16. Cool wort.

17. Add 2 gallons of cool water.

18. Siphon to fermenter.

19. Top up to 5 gallons.

20. Pitch yeast, and aerate wort.

21. Ferment at 68 degrees F.

Brew Note: You might wonder where the directions for bottling are in this recipe. As you proceed in your brewing experience, you will come across many recipes that make assumptions about what you, the home brewer, knows. One of the things that frequently will be omitted from recipes is bottling information. There are two reasons for this. The first reason is that, simply, it is assumed you know what you are doing. The ingredients list offers you a priming suggestion and leaves the rest to you. Second, you cannot assume that everyone who reads this recipe will bottle the beer. Many home brewers will keg their brews.

Dark Wheat Beer

5 gallons; OG = 1.055 to 1.056; FG = 1.011 to 1.012; IBU = 13

Ingredients:

Fermentables:

6 ¼ lbs. Muntons wheat dry malt extract (DME)

Specialty grains:

8 oz. German Munich malt

7 oz. Belgian cara-Munich malt

1 oz. British chocolate malt

Hops:

1 oz. Willamette bittering hops (4% alpha acid)

Yeast:

Wyeast 3056 (Bavarian Wheat Blend)

Primer:

1 ¼ cups Muntons wheat dry malt extract for priming

Directions:

1. Steep specialty grains in 1 gallon of 150-degree water for 30 minutes.

2. Remove steeped grains from brew pot, and rinse with 1 gallon of 170-degree water.

3. Add the dry malt, and stir well.

4. Bring the total volume in the brew pot to 2 ½ gallons.

5. Raise heat on brew pot, and bring to boil.

6. Add bittering hops.

7. Boil for 60 minutes.

8. Remove brew pot from heat.

9. Cool wort.

10. Strain into the primary fermenter, and add water to 5 gallons.

11. Pitch yeast when wort has cooled to below 80 degrees.

12. Aerate well.

13. Ferment at 68 degrees for two to three weeks.

Golden Light Ale

5 gallons; OG = 1.055; FG = 1.012; IBU = 32; ABV = 5.6%

Ingredients:

6 ⅗ lbs. Briess Golden Light LME

1 lb. Briess Bavarian Wheat LME

½ lb. crystal malt (10ºL)

1 oz. Northern Brewer (6.9%) 60 minutes

1 oz. Tettnanger (5.5% alpha acid) ten minutes

1 oz. Tettnanger (5.5% alpha acid) 0 minutes

Ferment with WLP001 (White Labs) California Ale Yeast

¾ cup corn sugar (priming)

Directions:

1. Heat 2 gallons of water to 152 degrees in a large brew pot.

2. Place specialty malt (crystal malt) in a steeping bag. Steep at 152 degrees.

3. Allow specialty grains to steep at 152 degrees for 60 minutes.

4. Heat 1 gallon of water in a large saucepan to 170 degrees.

5. Remove steeping bag from brew pot.

6. Place steeping bag in a large colander, and allow it to drain into brew pot.

7. Slowly rinse specialty grains with the 1 gallon of 170-degree water in the saucepan.

8. Add Briess Golden Light LME to brew pot, and stir well.

9. Raise heat on brew pot, and bring to a boil.

10. Follow hop schedule for a total boil of 60 minutes.

11. Do not let the wort volume go below 2 ¼ gallons. To do this, keep a kettle of water boiling separately that you might add during the 60-minute boil.

12. With ten minutes remaining in boil, remove brew pot from heat, and add Briess Bavarian Wheat LME.

13. Stir well.

14. Return to boil for remainder of 90-minute boil.

15. After 60 minutes, remove from heat, and make final hop addition.

16. Cool wort.

17. Add 2 gallons of cool water.

18. Siphon to fermenter.

19. Top up to 5 gallons.

20. Pitch yeast, and aerate wort.

21. Ferment at 68 degrees for two weeks.

22. Bottle condition with ¾ cup corn sugar for two weeks at 68 degrees.

Pitch Black Wild Rice Ale

This recipe is a good example of what can come with a little experimentation. It also serves as a good pre-step to the next chapter of intermediate brewing. This particular recipe began as a double India pale ale recipe employing extract and specialty grains. The addition of wild rice is a creative way to give the beer a slight nuttiness and highlight the high hop character.

This recipe will prepare you for the intermediate recipes in that the wild rice needs to be cooked and drained before using it in the wort. As you will see in the next section on intermediate brewing, this is something akin to the mash stage of partial mash brews.

5 gallons/19 L, extract with grains; OG = 1.064;
FG = 1.014; IBU = 65; ABV = 6.5%

Ingredients:

1 lb. (3 cups) Wild Rice

6 ½ lbs. Briess Light LME

1 lb. Briess Light DME

1 ½ lbs. caramel malt (10°L) crushed

1 lb. black malt (509°L) crushed

10 oz. Briess special roast malt (50°L) crushed

1 oz. Yakima Magnum hops (75 minutes) (14.1% alpha acid)

¼ oz. Cascade hops (2 minutes) (5.8% alpha acid)

¾ oz. Yakima Magnum hops (two minutes) (14.1% alpha acid)

¼ oz. Yakima Magnum hops (dry hops)

½ oz. Cascade hops (dry hops)

½ tsp. yeast nutrient (15 minutes)

½ tsp. Irish moss (30 minutes)

White Labs WLP001 (California Ale), Wyeast 1056 (American Ale)

¾ cup corn sugar (for priming)

Directions:

1. Rinse wild rice under running water until water runs clear.

2. Add wild rice to pot with 10 cups of cold water.

3. Bring rice to boil.

4. Reduce heat to simmer, and cover pot of rice.

5. Cook rice for 45 minutes.

6. Drain rice in a colander lined with a large piece of cheesecloth.

7. Tie corners of cheesecloth around wild rice making a large bag of rice.

8. Place crushed grains in a large steeping back, being careful not to pack them tightly.

9. Heat 2 gallons of water to 150 degrees.

10. Steep the crushed grain and wild rice in 2 gallons of water at 150 degrees for 30 minutes. Remove grains and wild rice from the wort.

11. Place wild rice and grain bags in a large colander, and place the colander over the wort pot.

12. Rinse with grains and wild rice with 2 quarts of 120-degree water, allowing the drained water to run into the wort.

13. Add the liquid malt extract to wort, and stir it in well, making sure it does not collect on the bottom of the pot.

14. Bring wort to boil, and boil for 75 minutes.

15. While boiling, add the hops, Irish moss, and yeast nutrient as per the schedule noted in the ingredients list.

16. During the boil, sanitize a fermenter.

17. Add the wort to 2 gallons of cold water in the sanitized fermenter.

18. Add cold water to bring the wort to 5 gallons.

19. Cool the wort to 75 degrees as quickly as possible using a wort chiller or by placing the fermenter in a sink full of ice.

20. Pitch your yeast.

21. Aerate the wort heavily by giving it a good stir.

22. Allow the beer to cool to 68 degrees.

23. Hold at that temperature until fermentation is complete (should take three to four days).

24. Transfer beer to a carboy using a siphon, avoiding any splashing to prevent aerating the beer.

25. Add the dry hops to the beer.

26. Allow the beer to condition for one week.

27. Bring 2 cups of water to boil in a small saucepan.

28. Dissolve priming sugar into the saucepan of boiling water for five minutes.

29. Pour sugar water mixture into a clean bottling bucket.

30. Carefully siphon beer from the fermenter to a bottling bucket.

31. Avoid transferring any sediment that might be at the bottom of the fermenter.

32. Use a bottling wand to fill bottles.

33. Allow the beer to carbonate, and age for at least two weeks.

CASE STUDY: SAMUEL MOORE:

I brewed my first batch of beer just before I turned 21 (don't tell the authorities!). I've been brewing about three and a half years.

I love good beer, I love chemistry, and I love cooking. As a chemical engineer and artisan beer enthusiast, brewing just came naturally. My brother-in-law helped me along, though. We brewed a batch together, and he "showed me the ropes" of brewing. After that, I found as many books as I could on the subject, and I have been deepening my knowledge ever since.

I brew 5-gallon batches of beer on a quarterly basis using recipes that I've designed or adapted. I love making anything from scratch, but enjoying a beer at the end of making something just seems so natural. My favorite part of brewing is the reward at the end. I occasionally brew root beer, ginger ale, and cider in 2-gallon batches. I'll often have friends over on brew days for a couple of extra hands, and I've taught a few of them how to brew this way.

I'm a hobbyist now, but I hope to brew commercially later in life. There are some laws established for hobbyists in Ohio: You cannot sell your beer at licensed retailers, and you can only brew a maximum of 500 gallons each year for personal consumption.

The hardest thing about brewing beer is working with 5 gallons of hot, boiling, sticky liquid. This is not only difficult but also dangerous. Unless you're a professional chef, you probably don't have the experience of moving around that amount of ingredients, and even a simple boil-over can become complicated very quickly.

I consider my beer to be a great success if it looks, smells, and tastes just how I planned. I've had a few failures in the past: over-carbonated beers, flat beers, beers with some unexpected flavors... but I can't say that I've ever made a beer I wasn't proud of.

A brewing method that I think those new to brewing should try is krausening.

Don't underestimate the power of krausening*. The ubiquitous method of bottle priming using corn syrup or a simple wort whipped up last-minute will work, but it's not really adding much to the beer in terms of flavor. Krausening adds a layer of depth to your beer just before it goes into bottles, and it showcases the hops aroma that otherwise would have been stripped by the carbon dioxide vent in primary fermentation. It's a lot easier than books make it out to be.

My favorite beer to brew is Russian imperial stout. I brew a Russian imperial stout most often, but my recipe is constantly adapting.

My favorite style to drink is the American wild ale. Somewhere between a wine and a beer, this style really showcases the flexibility and the potential range of flavors in beer. But really, my favorite beer to drink is the one I have not yet tried!

The most common mistake brewers of all degrees of experience make is too much or too little focus on the precision of brewing. Beer is very forgiving. Sanitation is extremely important if you don't want sour or rustic flavors in your beer. However, you can make a very palatable beer without any sanitation at all. You have to pick a route and act accordingly. Other than that, problems such as a wrong hops or yeast variety, a high fermentation temperature, or low sugar yield in your mash just add to the unique qualities of your beer. Just like in cooking, the same recipe doesn't have to taste the same every time you make it.

My words of advice to those new to brewing are: Do NOT buy the "beer in a can" kit. That's like buying microwave easy mac and expecting homemade macaroni and cheese. Head to your local home-brew supply shop, and chat with the people there. These shops usually have pre-assembled beginner kits that give you an idea of what type of supplies you'll need. Ironically, a cheap and easy way to see if you'll like brewing beer is to brew a couple of gallons of root beer or ginger ale first and bottle prime with brewer's yeast. It will take a lot less time than a full beer-brewing day. You can make smaller batches, you'll learn how to handle a large amount of boiling liquid, you'll become acquainted with brewer's yeast and bottling, the root beer will be ready in only a few days versus a month, and the equipment you'll purchase can be used for brewing beer as well.

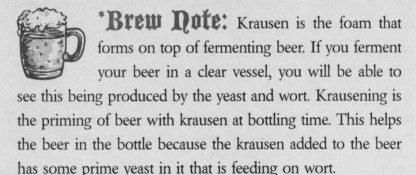 ***Brew Note:** Krausen is the foam that forms on top of fermenting beer. If you ferment your beer in a clear vessel, you will be able to see this being produced by the yeast and wort. Krausening is the priming of beer with krausen at bottling time. This helps the beer in the bottle because the krausen added to the beer has some prime yeast in it that is feeding on wort.

There are numerous ways to achieve this process, but the difficult part of this process is having fresh krausen at bottling time. Because krausen is produced in the brew early in the fermentation process, you will have to brew up a smaller batch of fresh wort to have krausen on hand to bottle prime with or be in the process of brewing another batch of the same beer when you plan on bottling.

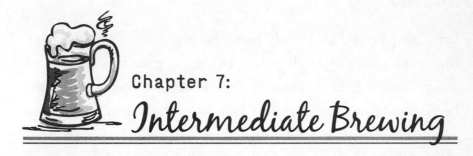

Chapter 7:
Intermediate Brewing

I f you have made several batches of beer from the recipes provided in the previous chapter and/or from ingredient kits you obtained from a home-brew retailer, you have gotten a good education on brewing beer using malt extracts. Extract brewing is fun and produces good results if you use clean equipment and follow the directions closely. However, now you might be longing to take the next step in brewing and proceed on to brewing all-grain. That is, brewing without the malt extract.

Jumping from extract brewing to all-grain brewing can be a daunting task. If you have been reading home-brewing magazines or online forums about all-grain brewing, you probably are thinking you are going to need to get some new equipment and, in many ways, relearn the brewing process. To the beginning extract brewer, the

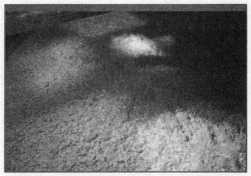

Mash cooking up in a large brewery.

world of all-grain brewing can seem like being in a foreign land. This is not the case.

Let it first be said that many home brewers never make the jump from extract brewing to all-grain brewing. All-grain brewing is more complicated and time consuming than extract brewing is, and many home brewers cannot make that kind of commitment. Experienced extract brewers still are able to produce creative and complex beers using the wide variety of malt extracts available to the home brewer. These brewers have moved beyond using home-brew ingredient kits and have developed excellent recipes by mixing the component parts of a wide array of beer styles.

Although many home brewers never make the leap from extract brewing to all-grain brewing, many of them do operate in the middle ground of brewing that is neither all extract nor all grain. This brewing technique is known as the partial mash.

Mash, as you recall from Chapter 1, is a fermentable starchy mixture from which alcohol, in this case beer, can be brewed or distilled. This verb, to mash, is to convert malt or grain into this mixture. To mash is to steep the grain (the base malts) in hot water, which activates the malt enzymes and converts the grain starches into fermentable sugars. Malt extract is base malt that already has undergone the mashing stage. Partial mash occurs when a brewer combines an extract with a measure of home-mashed base malt.

The best way to make the transition from extract and specialty grain brewing to all-grain brewing is to take the intermediate step of doing a partial mash. Learning to work with the mash gives you the experience of the procedure without having to work with the quantity of mash you will have to employ in an all-grain recipe.

Intermediate Ingredients

The ingredients needed to take the step from extract and specialty grain brewing to partial mash brewing are merely the addition of base malt. You will remember from Chapter 3 that malts are divided into two categories, base malts and specialty malts. Base malts are the primary source of the diastatic power in any recipe. Diastatic power is the enzymatic power of the malt. This defines the malt's power to break down starches into even fermentable sugars during the mashing process. The word "diastatic" is used in reference to "diastase" enzymes.

Base malts are the primary malt in any recipe. There are three important things to know about these malts:

1) **Must be mashed** — Base malts must be mashed to convert their starch into fermentable sugars and dextrins. Mashing continues the enzymatic breakdown that was begun during the malting process. Mashing breaks down the long-chain sugars to enable the yeast to consume them during fermentation.

2) **Diastatic power** — Base malts are higher in enzymes than specialty malts. The roasting process that the specialty malts go through destroys much of their diastatic power.

3) **Fully modified** — Most base malt varieties have been fully modified to allow them sufficient enzymatic viability. This means that they are able mash both themselves and 20 to 40 percent of adjuncts or non-enzymatic grains.

You will come across four kinds of base malt most often in the partial mash and all-grain recipes you will brew. Other base malts are available, but the four noted here are the primary ingredients to a world of beer styles.

North American two-row

North American two-row malt is pale-colored domestic malt (less than 2 degrees Lovibond) and has a relatively high level of protein (12 to 13 percent). Six-row and two-row describe the physical arrangement of kernels on the barley plant. Two-row barley has higher starch content than six-row barley and will yield a greater amount of malt extract.

North American six-row

North American pale-colored six-row malt (less than 2 degrees Lovibond). The six-row malt is also high in protein. Six-row barley is more adaptable than other varieties of the grain to a wider variety of climates and is somewhat easier to grow. It has slightly less enzyme potential than two-row and slightly more extract potential. It is used as the main base malt in a wide range of beer styles. Produced by maltsters to big brewery specifications, this malt will support high levels of adjunct.

Traditional Bohemian pilsner

Traditional Bohemian pilsner is darker than domestic malt varieties (about 3 to 4 degrees Lovibond). This base malt will give beer a golden color and a dry mouthfeel. Mouthfeel in beer is defined as the discernment of body as the result of proteins and dextrins, or sugars. Not as common as North American two-row malt, but this malt is making a bit of a comeback. Samuel Adams brewers recently have begun using this malt for their Samuel Adams Noble Pils.

British pale ale malt

British pale ale malt is darker (4 degrees Lovibond) than the more common North American two-row malt. This malt will result in a darker color beer than the beer made with American two-row or six-row malt. It also will give beer a maltier and biscuitier flavor.

Intermediate Brewing Equipment

The most important piece of equipment you will need to think about as you approach the partial mash of intermediate brewing is something called a mash lauter tun. This hybrid piece of equipment combines a mash tun and a lauter tun. Mashing is the process of converting malted barley into a fermentable liquid. The tun is the vessel in which this process is accomplished. Lautering is the brewing stage in which the mash liquid is separated from the spent grain. To accomplish this task in the most efficient way possible, it is not only important to run the liquid mash off of the grain, but to rinse the grain and get as much of the extract sugars as possible. You will remember that this rinsing is called sparging. For simplicity sake at this intermediate level, you can consider your mash tun and lautering tun the same vessel.

As a novice brewer, even as a novice intermediate brewer, chances are that you will not run out and buy a good quality mash lauter tun. The starting price for an 8-gallon mash lauter tun is about $250.

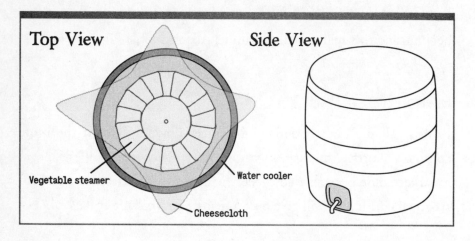

You can build a mash lauter tun from an insulated cooler or cooler drink dispenser. Until recently, this option might not have been a good idea, as the plastic used to construct these items was considered unsafe. However, in the last couple of years, many manufacturers of these items have changed the plastic used, and now home brewers easily can make their own inexpensive mash lauter tuns.

If you would like to build a mash lauter tun on your own, it is important that you understand the principle of mashing and lautering. The basic tasks that need to be accomplished by this piece of equipment are the mashing of the base malt and specialty malts for at least half an hour at temperatures from 150 to 160 degrees. Following this mash, the system needs to be drained without getting clogged and rinsed, again without getting clogged.

The reason that 5- and 10-gallon insulated drink dispensers are perfect for this task is that they are large enough to hold the amount of water and grain you will be using. These vessels will hold the mash at a fairly constant temperature for an extended period. Finally, these vessels are built with spigots at the base that make them easy to drain from the bottom.

The most basic design for an insulated drink dispenser mash lauter tun is one that has a perforated false bottom inside that sits about an inch off the bottom of the vessel. The grain sits on the false bottom and the water runs through the grain, through the false bottom, and out the spigot. Both the false bottom and the grain act to strain the wort.

A simple system to use in an insulated drink dispenser is to set a circular vegetable steamer on the floor of the dispenser. The spigot of the dispenser should be below the vegetable steamer. These steamers can be purchased in grocery stores and are built to fit inside of medium to large saucepans. Then, purchase two packs of standard cheesecloth. Line the inside of the drink dispenser with the cheesecloth so that it sits on top of the vegetable steamer and comes up outside of the top of mash lauter tun. You can use a large rubber band to secure the cheesecloth. You have now fitted the inside of the tun with a large grain bag. The cheesecloth is light enough that you will be able to securely close the lid of the dispenser. This setup will allow you to mash a rather large quantity of grain (certainly enough for any partial mash recipe).

You also could fashion your own custom-made false bottom out of stainless steel that fits snuggly inside the insulated drink dispenser. This would eliminate the need for cheesecloth. Beyond this, you might replace the spigot of the insulated drink dispenser with brass fittings and a valve that might be a little more user friendly than the push-button valve on the insulated drink dispenser.

Another type of design that is relatively common for these homemade mash lauter tuns employs a manifold system that sits on the bottom of the insulated drink dispenser or cooler. These manifold systems are pipes or tubes perforated with holes or slots that allow mash to flow out but keep the grain in the vessel. These systems are a little more complicated to manufacture, but they are not beyond the capabilities of those of you who are good with tools.

You can find many good designs to a variety of homemade mash lauter tuns online. A good place to start is John Palmer's "How to Brew" website at **www.howtobrew.com/appendices/appendixD.html**. The design noted here is for a mash lauter tun that uses a manifold system.

For an even simpler design, you can go to **www.byo.com/stories/projects-and-equipment/article/indices/20-build-it-yourself/399-build-your-own-mashlauter-tun**. This design is for a system that uses two buckets, one inside of the other.

If you look around online, you will be able to find something that suits your needs and budget. The most important thing to know before you proceed is what the system needs to accomplish. Once you have that, you are well on your creative way to manufacturing your own mash lauter tun.

If you are not a handy individual, or if you would rather just purchase a pre-made plastic mash lauter tun, you can get a 5-gallon tun through your local home-brew retailer or through online home-brew retailers for about $120.

From here on, the recipes are noted using the terms cooler and mash lauter tun interchangeably. The reason for this is that this is the most cost-effective way for new home brewers to operate. The recent changes in the type of plastics that these coolers are made with allow home brewers to use them safely as affordable brewing equipment. When a recipe states "water should be added to the cooler," it is implied that the cooler is the mash lauter tun.

Do the Partial Mash

The great thing about graduating from extract brewing to partial mash brewing, as opposed to jumping directly to all-grain brewing from extract brewing, is that a partial mash is begun exactly the same way as the mash portion of all-grain brewing. The differences in the two methods are in the quantity of grain used and in the fact that you will still get much of your fermentable wort using an extract. What the partial mash will give you in the end is a beer that has a greater complexity than beer made from just an extract and a few specialty grains.

A partial mash is handled in exactly the same way as a full mash, except for the fact that you will only be dealing with about 3 ½ gallons of wort as opposed to about 7 gallons in an all-grain full mash. The wort you collect in a partial mash will contribute more to the personality of the beer. The wort you collect in an all-grain full mash will contribute all of the fermentables.

The best way to describe this process is to do so in the form of a recipe. The recipe that will be used for this explanation of a partial mash is one for imperial oatmeal stout. The reason this recipe is good for this purpose is that it is quite difficult to make oatmeal stout without doing a partial mash. The mash stage of this recipe is vital, as the oats need to be mashed with barley to convert the starches in the oats to sugar.

This recipe will be explained in the stages of the process that make up the partial mash. Those stages are the mash in, collecting the wort, sparging, collecting the second wort, boiling (the stage where extract and hops are added), and fermenting. You see by the list of stages that the first four stages take the place of steeping the grains. After these initial stages, the process is the same as it is for an extract brew.

Imperial Oatmeal Stout

The title "imperial" in a beer style indicates that this brew has a little (or sometimes a lot) more than the traditional style type. This imperial stout has quite a bit more roasted maltiness and a much higher ABV than your average stout. Some imperial stouts also have a higher IBU. This one is rated at about 43, which is in the moderate category for an imperial stout, but dry stout will range from 30 to 35 IBU and sweet stout will range from 15 to 25 IBU.

Another style of beer that often carries the "imperial" moniker is India pale ale. Imperial pale ale has a much higher IBU score than the traditional IPA and usually has a much higher ABV score, as well.

Total batch size = 5 gallons; partial mash in 3-gallon insulated drink cooler/dispenser; ~3-gallon 60-minute stove-top boil; late malt extract addition; target ABV of 9%; 43 IBU (target OG: 1.090; target FG: 1.021)

 Brew Note: This brew will require the brewer to use a blow-off hose as opposed to an airlock during primary fermentation. It is an extremely active brew.

Note the slight difference in the ingredient list compared to the ingredients in an extract with grains recipe. In the ingredient list below, the 1 lb. pale malt is the base malt used in this partial mash. Along with the base malt are the specialty malts: roasted barley, black malt, chocolate malt, and caramel crystal

Quick cooking rolled oats

malt. In addition to the malts that will be used in this mash is 1 lb. of oats (as this is an oatmeal stout recipe).

Ingredients:

1 lb. pale malt (two-row)

½ lb. roasted barley

1 lb. black (patent) malt34

1 lb. chocolate malt

1 lb. caramel crystal malt (80ºL)

1 lb. McCann's Quick Cooking Rolled Oats

This is a hefty amount of malt extract. The 9 lbs of DME noted here is an indication that this brew is an imperial stout. The DME in this recipe provides most of the fermentables in this brew.

6 lbs. Briess Traditional Dark Dry Malt Extract (DME)

3 lbs. Briess Traditional Dark Dry Malt Extract (DME)

1 ½ oz. Chinook (12.2% AA)

1 oz. Nugget (13%)

1 tsp. Irish Moss (15 minutes)

½ tsp. yeast nutrient (15 minutes)

Wyeast Irish Ale Yeast (1084)

4 oz. corn sugar (optional for bottle priming)

Hop Schedule:

1 ½ oz. Chinook — 60 minute boil

1 oz. Nugget — 25 minute boil

The Mash In

The first six steps of this recipe are what is referred to as the mash in. This is the stage you will heat the mash water to a given temperature (in this case 166 degrees) and then transfer the hot water to your mash lauter tun. It is here when the enzymatic breakdown of starches into sugars occurs.

You can do this stage using a grain-steeping bag, or you may allow the grains to mash loosely in the mash lauter tun. If you will be considering a move to all-grain brewing, you should try to allow the grains to mash loosely, as this is how you will have to perform an all-grain mash.

Your mash lauter tun might also dictate whether you should use a steeping bag. If your equipment is not prepared to do a loose grain mash, you will need a way to steep the grains.

1. In a large pot, heat 2 gallons of water to 166 degrees for a target mash temperature of 154 degrees.

2. Pour the hot water into a cooler.

3. Place the 4 ½ pounds of crushed grain (pale, barley, black, chocolate) and 1 pound of oats into a large steeping bag, or pour loosely into a mash lauter tun.

4. Slowly lower the grain-steeping bag into the water, or pour the grains slowly into the water.

5. Gently agitate the steeping bag, or stir the grains with a large spoon, or paddle to ensure all the grain is steeping.

6. Cover the cooler, and allow the steeping grains to rest 60 minutes.

Collecting the wort

As the mash is nearing completion, heat ½ gallon of water to boil in your brew pot. Heat another gallon of water to about 180 degrees in a large saucepan (this water will be your sparge, or rinse, water.)

The initial mash stage will be completed after 60 minutes for this particular recipe, though some recipes might call for a longer mash time. Use a heavy-duty saucepan with a reliable handle or any other similar container that can handle hot liquid, and draw a quart of wort from the mash lauter tun through the spigot. Be careful, as it will still be about 150 degrees. Carefully pour this wort back into the mash lauter tun, over the grain or the steeping bag. Repeat this procedure several times until the wort runs free of husks or grain pieces. You only should need to recirculate two or three quarts of wort for things to run free.

Once you have fairly free running wort, open the spigot, and draw off all the wort that runs off from the mash lauter tun. Immediately pour this wort into the ½ gallon of boiling water in your brew pot. Pouring the wort into the boiling water will halt the enzymatic activity of the wort and "fix" its fermentability. In a full mash, this process is known as the mash out and is the other side of the mash in. Allow this mash to boil in your brew pot as you continue with your sparge stage.

Note the number of times the word "gently" is used when the direction calls for pouring the wort. This is an important word to underline, as excessive splashing will tend to aerate the wort at a time when you do not want to aerate it. Aerating the wort at this stage could have negative consequences down the line because it could result in long-term oxidation, which will lead to an off flavor in the beer.

Sparge

Simply put, sparging is rinsing the grain and collecting the sugars produced during the mash in the rinse runoff while leaving the grain matter behind. The sugars are collected by the rinse, or sparge.

There are several methods of sparging from which to choose: fly sparging, no sparging, and batch sparging. Fly sparging involves continuously introducing heated water to the grain bed, usually by spraying it, to rinse off the grain. The no sparge is similar to what you do using a grain steep bag as you simply drain the wort from the grain bag or bed. Batch sparging is the method preferred by many home brewers that brew using the homemade cooler mash lauter tun.

The batch sparge is accomplished by first recirculating the wort through the mash lauter tun until the runoff runs clear of sediment. Rinsing with heated clean water follows this recirculation. The heated clean water is collected, as it contains sugars produced during the mash, and added to the wort boiling in the brew pot.

1. As the grains mash in the mash lauter tun, heat a gallon of water to 180 degrees (this water will be used for sparging.)

2. Near the end of the 60-minute steeping period, heat 2 quarts of water to a boil in your brew pot. (You now have three vessels going: the mash lauter tun; water for sparge; water in brew pot.)

3. After the first mash is complete (60 minutes), remove the mash lauter tun lid.

4. Open the spigot of the cooler to draw off 1 quart of wort into saucepan.

5. Gently and slowly pour the drawn wort back into the mash lauter tun over the steeping grain bag or loose grains. Try to avoid splashing any of the liquid.

6. Slowly draw off the wort by the pan-full, and carefully pour that wort into the boiling water in your brew pot.

7. After you have drawn the wort off from the mash lauter tun, carefully add the hot (180 degree) water to the top of the mash lauter tun (this keeps the grains and oats submerged in water that is about 165 degrees).

8. After 1 gallon has been added to the steeped grains in the mash lauter tun, cover the mash lauter tun, and let it rest for ten minutes.

9. Slowly draw off all of the wort from the mash lauter tun, and add it to your brew pot. (You should have about 3 ½ gallons of wort in your brew pot.)

From this point on the procedure is the same as doing a brew with extracts as was explained in Chapter 5.

10. When the wort in the brew pot is at a rolling boil, add hops according to the schedule indicated in the ingredients list.

11. Thirty minutes into the boil, begin slowly adding 6 lbs. DME, stirring well to dissolve.

12. With 15 minutes remaining in the boil, stir in 1 tsp. of Irish Moss and ½ tsp. of yeast nutrient.

13. Remove pot from boil after 60 minutes.

14. Add remaining 3 lbs. DME.

15. Cover pot, and allow the wort to rest for ten to 15 minutes.

16. Cool wort as quickly as possible to about 80 degrees.

17. Transfer wort to a primary fermenter.

18. Add cool water to wort to bring the total volume to 5 gallons.

19. Use a cleaned and sanitized hydrometer to check the OG.

20. Stir well to aerate.

21. Pitch yeast, and aerate well by stirring.

22. Ferment in primary for one week.

23. Transfer to secondary for two weeks.

24. Allow the beer to bottle condition for at least three weeks.

Chapter 8:
Partial Mash Recipes

here are a good variety of partial mash recipes. All of these recipes employ the same techniques explained in Chapter 7.

Partial Mash Chocolate Cherry Stout

Chapter 3 described the use of a variety of adjuncts to flavor beer. One of the more popular adjuncts used in brewing is fruit. This recipe uses two kinds of cherries to make a chocolate stout that might serve well as a dessert brew.

When using the cherries in this recipe, you can choose whether to use them with or without the pits. The pits will give the beer a more complex almond-like flavor.

Do not be surprised by the renewed fermentation activity after the cherries are added. The fruit has a pretty good supply of natural sugar that the yeast will love.

5 gallons; OG = 1.056; FG = 1.020; IBU = 30; ABV = 4.75%

Ingredients:

6 ⅗ lbs. (two cans) Briess light unhopped LME

1 lb. Munich malt (10ºL)

1 lb. wheat malt

4 oz. roasted barley malt

4 oz. chocolate malt

1 lb. McCann's Irish Quick Cooking Oats

1 ½ oz. Goldings hops (4.75% alpha acid) 60 min.

1 tsp. Irish moss (boil 15 minutes)

1 tsp. yeast nutrient (boil 15 minutes)

1 oz. Goldings hops (4.75% alpha acid) 5 min.

5 lbs. Bing cherries (crushed)

1 lb. red tart pie cherries (crushed)

Wyeast 1968 (London ESB) or White Labs WLP002 (English Ale) yeast

¾ cup corn sugar (for priming)

Directions:

1. In a large pot, heat 1 ½ gallons of water to 162 degrees for a target mash temperature of 150 degrees.

2. Pour the hot water into a cooler.

3. Place the 3 ½ lbs. of crushed grain (Munich, wheat, barley, chocolate, and oats) into a large steeping bag or pour loosely into a mash lauter tun.

4. Slowly lower the grain-steeping bag into the water.

5. Gently agitate the steeping bag with a large spoon, or paddle to ensure all the grain is steeping.

6. Cover the cooler, and allow the steeping grains to rest 60 minutes.

7. As the grains mash in the mash lauter tun, heat a gallon of water to 180 degrees. (This water will be used for sparging.)

8. Near the end of the 60-minute steeping period, heat 2 quarts of water to a boil in your brew pot.

9. After the first mash is complete (60 minutes), remove the mash lauter tun lid.

10. Open the spigot of the cooler to draw off 1 quart of wort into saucepan.

11. Gently and slowly pour the drawn wort back into the mash lauter tun over the steeping grain bag or loose grains. Try to avoid splashing any of the liquid.

12. Slowly draw off the wort by the pan-full, and carefully pour that wort into the boiling water in your brew pot.

13. After you have drawn the wort off from the mash lauter tun, carefully add the hot (180-degree) water to the top of the mash lauter tun.

14. After 1 gallon has been added to the steeped grains in the mash lauter tun, cover the mash lauter tun, and let it rest for ten minutes.

15. Slowly draw off all of the wort from the mash lauter tun, and add it to your brew pot. (You should have about 2 ¾ gallons of wort in your brew pot.)

16. When the wort in the brew pot is at a rolling boil, add hops according to the schedule indicated in the ingredients list.

17. Thirty minutes into the boil, begin slowly adding the LME, stirring well to dissolve.

18. With 15 minutes remaining in the boil, stir in 1 tsp. of Irish Moss and ½ tsp. of yeast nutrient.

19. Remove pot from boil after 60 minutes.

20. Cover pot, and allow the wort to rest ten to 15 minutes.

21. Cool wort as quickly as possible to about 80 degrees.

22. Transfer wort to a primary fermenter.

23. Add cool water to wort to bring the total volume to 5 gallons.

24. Use a cleaned and sanitized hydrometer to check the OG.

25. Stir well to aerate.

26. Pitch yeast, and aerate well by stirring.

27. Ferment in primary for one week.

28. Add cherries to secondary fermenter.

29. Transfer beer to secondary fermenter on top of cherries for two weeks.

30. Transfer beer to carboy for a week before bottling.

31. Allow the beer to bottle condition for at least three weeks.

American Cream Ale

Here is a great partial mash recipe for a light, creamy American classic. Everything about this beer is light, from its taste to its bitterness and alcohol content. This is the perfect post-Saturday afternoon lawn-mowing beer or beer in the cooler for a Sunday picnic.

5 gallon, OG = 1.044; FG = 1.008; IBU = 15; ABV = 4.6%

This interpretation of American cream ale uses the classic American hop, Cluster. Fifty percent of the extract weight comes from the mini-mash.

Ingredients:

3 lbs. pale malt (two-row)

1 lb. flaked maize

1 lb. corn sugar

3 ⅓ lbs. Briess Pilsen Light liquid malt extract (late addition)

½ oz. Cluster hops (60 minutes) (7% alpha acids)

1 oz. Irish moss (15 minutes)

¼ tsp. yeast nutrients (15 minutes)

Wyeast 1056 (American Ale), White Labs WLP001 (California Ale)

1 cup corn sugar (for priming)

Directions:

1. Heat 5 ½ qts. of water to 163 degrees.
2. Transfer heated water to mash lauter tun.

3. Mash maize and crushed grains at 152 degrees for 45 minutes.

4. Bring ½ gallon of water to boil in a brew pot.

5. Recirculate, run off first wort (a little more than a gallon).

6. Heat 1 gallon of water to 185 degrees in a large saucepan. (This will be your sparge water.)

7. Collect first wort, and transfer it to ½ gallon of boiling water in your brew pot.

8. Gently add 185-degree sparge water to mash lauter tun.

9. Allow grains in mash lauter tun to rest for five minutes.

10. Recirculate wort in mash lauter tun.

11. Run off second wort, and gently add to brew pot. (You now have about 2 ¾ gallons of wort in the brew pot.)

12. Bring wort to a boil.

13. Add corn sugar and bittering hops to wort.

14. Boil for 60 minutes.

15. Add Irish moss and yeast nutrients to wort with 15 minutes left in boil.

16. After 60 minutes, remove wort from heat.

17. Stir in LME and cover brew pot.

18. Allow wort to rest for 15 minutes.

19. Cool wort as quickly as possible.

20. Transfer wort to fermenter.

21. Add cool water to bring wort volume to 5 gallons.

22. When wort reaches 72 to 68 degrees, aerate, and pitch yeast.

23. Ferment at 68 degrees for one week in primary fermenter.

24. Transfer to secondary fermenter and ferment for two weeks in secondary.

25. Bottle condition with 1 cup of corn sugar.

Partial Mash Blonde Ale

5 gallons; OG = 1.047 FG = 1.011; IBU = 23; ABV = 4.6%

Ingredients:

5 lbs. Breiss Golden Light DME

1 lb. pale malt (two-row)

½ lb. CaraPils® malt

1 oz. Cascade hops (45 minutes) (6% alpha acid)

½ oz. Liberty hops (ten minutes) (4.5% alpha acid)

½ oz. Liberty hops (0 minutes) (0.5 oz./14.2 g of 4.5% alpha acid)

Wyeast 1056 (American Ale), 1007 (German Ale), White Labs WLP001 (California Ale) or WLP 029 (German Ale) yeast

½ tsp. yeast nutrient

¾ cup corn sugar (for priming)

Directions:

1. Heat 1 gallon of water to 165 degrees.

2. Transfer heated water to mash lauter tun.

3. Mash crushed grains at 160 degrees for 30 minutes.

4. Bring 1 ½ gallons of water to boil in a brew pot.

5. Recirculate, run off first wort (a little more than a gallon).

6. Heat 1 ½ qts. of water to 170 degrees in a large saucepan. (This will be your sparge water.)

7. Collect first wort, and transfer it to 1 ½ gallons of boiling water in your brew pot.

8. Gently add 170-degree sparge water to mash lauter tun.

9. Allow grains in mash lauter tun to rest for five minutes.

10. Recirculate wort in mash lauter tun.

11. Run off second wort, and gently add to brew pot. (You now have about 3 gallons of wort in the brew pot).

12. Bring wort to a boil.

13. Add DME and Cascade (bittering) hops to wort.

14. Boil for 45 minutes.

15. After 35 minutes, add ½ oz. Liberty hops and yeast nutrient.

16. After 45 minutes, remove wort from heat.

17. Add ½ oz. Liberty hops.

18. Cool wort as quickly as possible to about 80 degrees.

19. Transfer wort to fermenter.

20. Add cool water to bring wort volume to 5 gallons.

21. When wort reaches 72 to 68 degrees, aerate, and pitch yeast.

22. Ferment at 70 degrees for two weeks in primary fermenter.

23. Transfer to secondary fermenter for two weeks.

24. Bottle condition with ¾ cup of corn sugar.

Austrian Lager

Lager is the most popular beer style in the world because of its refreshing and thirst-quenching appeal. Popular commercial beers such as Budweiser, Miller Genuine Draft, and Coors are all lagers.

This is the first lager-style beer recipe described here; so a few additional notes of explanation are required related to the fermentation process. Recall from Chapter 2 that lager is a bottom-fermented beer that is fermented at cooler temperatures than the top-fermented ales described above. Lagers have a much crisper taste than the top-fermented ales. Lagers are the most difficult beers for novice home brewers to make because they demand a steady, cool fermentation and extended refrigeration during the aging process. The distinct flavor of lagers is achieved by fermenting for longer periods.

You will note some new terminology near the conclusion of this recipe. Previous ale recipes have called for primary and, in some cases, secondary fermentation. The primary fermentation in the brewing of lager needs to be watched closely. You will observe the activity of the airlock, and when the airlock remains inactive for a 48-hour period, you can consider the primary fermentation complete.

This recipe directs you to a primary fermentation, followed by a diacetyl rest, and then a stage called lager. The diacetyl rest is a period of about three days that you will leave the beer in the fermenter after the completion of fermentation. During fermentation, the yeast release a number of byproducts into your beer, one of them being diacetyl, a naturally occurring chemical. During the stage called diacetyl rest, the yeast will re-absorb the diacetyl they have produced and thus take it back out of your beer. Diacetyl is not usually a problem with ale because it is fermented at a higher temperature and the yeast more readily re-absorb the chemical at the warmer temperatures. However, with lagers, if you do not allow for the diacetyl rest, your beer will retain the unabsorbed diacetyl and probably will acquire a somewhat buttery flavor. Diacetyl is commonly used as a flavoring in buttered popcorn and other products that require that particular flavor, but buttery beer is generally not what you will be brewing.

The final stage of the lager fermentation process is the stage called lagering. This stage can be done before or after the beer is bottled and is, perhaps, better referred to as conditioning rather than fermentation.

As previously mentioned, bottom-fermenting lager yeast ferments at lower temperatures than the top-fermenting ale yeasts. Low fermentation temperatures and extended maturation times result in beer with a purer and crisper flavor than its top-fermented ale cousin. The extended cold conditioning (lagering) also makes these beers more shelf-stable than ales. This extended shelf life is one reason why most of the world's beers are lagers.

You can lager a brew either before or after you have bottled it. To bottle condition before lagering, you wait until the beer has completed fermentation and had its diacetyl rest. Then, prime the beer with corn sugar or DME as you normally would when bottling ale. Allow the beer to carbonate in the bottle at room temperature for a week. At this point, open a bottle to make sure it is carbonated. If it is not yet carbonated, give it three or four more days and try opening one again. The beer should be carbonated at room temperature because once it is moved to a cold storage, it will not carbonate further. After you are sure that carbonation is complete, move it to cold storage from 32 to 42 degrees to lager it. It is best to drop the temperature in several stages if you can; allow it several days at 60 degrees, several days at 50 degrees, and then down to 32 to 42 degrees. The lagering stage can last anywhere from 4 weeks to 6 months, depending on beer style and brewer patience.

Alternatively, you can bottle the beer after the lagering is complete.

Having a place to store beer at these temperatures is difficult for many home brewers. This is the reason many brewers stick to brewing ales. Good places to lager beer are extra refrigerators or basements and outside storage places in the winter.

Lagering before bottling is something akin to the secondary fermentation, though it is done at a much lower temperature. This lagering might take four weeks to a few months depending on the beer. The yeast in this lagered beer becomes inactive for such an extended period, it is suggested that you add fresh yeast when it comes time to bottle the beer. Generally, ¼ pack of yeast (about ½ tsp.) should be enough to do the job.

This Austrian Lager recipe will produce:

  5 gallon; OG = 1.051; FG = 1.013; IBU = 20; ABV = 5.0%

Ingredients:

3 ½ lbs. Vienna malt

½ lb. CaraMunich II malt (45 °L)

1 oz. chocolate malt

¾ lb. Briess Light dried malt extract

4 lbs. light liquid malt extract (late addition)

1 ¼ oz. Spalt hops (60 minutes) (4% alpha acids)

¼ oz. Hallertau Mittelfrueh hops (ten minutes) (4% alpha acids)

1 tsp. Irish moss (15 minutes)

Wyeast 2206 (Bavarian Lager), White Labs WLP820 (Octoberfest/
Märzen)

¾ cup corn sugar (for priming)

Directions:

1. Heat 5.5 qts. water to 167 degrees.

2. Transfer 167-degree water to mash lauter tun.

3. Add grains to mash lauter tun, and mash at 154 degrees for 45 minutes.

4. Bring ½ gallon of water to boil in a brew pot.

5. Recirculate, run off first wort (a little more than a gallon).

6. Heat 1 gallon of water to 185 degrees in a large saucepan. (This will be your sparge water.)

7. Collect first wort, and transfer it to ½ gallon of boiling water in your brew pot.

8. Gently add 185-degree sparge water to mash lauter tun.

9. Allow grains in mash lauter tun to rest for five minutes.

10. Recirculate wort in mash lauter tun.

11. Run off second wort, and gently add to brew pot. (You now have about 2 ¾ gallons of wort in the brew pot.)

12. Add DME to wort in brew pot.

13. Bring wort to a boil.

14. Add hops and Irish moss as indicated on ingredient list.

15. Add LME to wort with 15 minutes remaining in boil (Do this by removing brew pot from heat and stirring the LME in well before returning brew pot to heat and boil.)

16. Cool wort as quickly as possible to 52 to 58 degrees. (Adding cold water to bring the wort volume to 5 gallons can help reach this temperature.)

17. Transfer wort to a cleaned and sanitized fermenter.

18. Ferment at 54 degrees until fermentation is complete.

19. Diacetyl rest at 60 degrees for three days.

20. Lager at 40 degrees.

ESB (Extra Special Bitter)

5 gallon; OG = 1.045; FG = 1.011; IBU = 34; ABV = 4.4%

ESB is wonderful all-purpose ale because of the nearly perfect balance of malt and hop flavor and bitterness. This beer goes with just about any food at any time.

Ingredients:

3 ¼ lbs. pale malt (two-row)

1 lb. crystal malt (60°L)

½ lb. Briess Golden Light DME

3 ³⁄₁₀ lbs. Briess Golden Light LME (late addition)

1 ½ oz. Fuggle hops (60 minutes) (5% alpha acids)

⅔ oz. E.K. Goldings hops (15 minutes) (5% alpha acids)

⅔ oz. E.K. Goldings hops (two minutes) (5% alpha acids)

1 tsp. Irish moss

Wyeast 1968 (London ESB) or White Labs WLP002 (English Ale)

¾ cup corn sugar (for priming)

Directions:

1. Heat 5 ½ quarts of water to 165 degrees.

2. Transfer heated water to mash lauter tun.

3. Mash crushed grains at 154 degrees for 30 minutes.

4. Bring ¾ gallon of water to boil in a brew pot.

5. Recirculate, run off first wort (a little more than a gallon).

6. Heat 5 ½ qts. of water to 180 degrees in a large saucepan. (This will be your sparge water.)

7. Collect first wort, and transfer it to ¾ gallon of boiling water in your brew pot.

8. Gently add 180-degree sparge water to mash lauter tun.

9. Allow grains in mash lauter tun to rest for five minutes.

10. Recirculate wort in mash lauter tun.

11. Run off second wort, and gently add to brew pot (you now have about 3 ¼ gallons of wort in the brew pot).

12. Bring wort to a boil.

13. Add DME and bittering hops to wort.

14. Boil for 60 minutes.

15. After 45 minutes, remove wort from heat.

16. Add Irish moss, flavoring hops, and LME to wort with 15 minutes left in boil.

17. Return wort to boil.

18. Add Aroma hops to wort with two minutes remaining in boil.

19. Remove wort for heat after a total boil of 60 minutes.

20. Cool wort as quickly as possible to about 80 degrees.

21. Transfer wort to fermenter.

22. Add cool water to bring wort volume to 5 gallons.

23. When wort reaches 72 to 68 degrees, aerate, and pitch yeast.

24. Ferment at 70 degrees for two weeks in primary fermenter.

25. Bottle condition with ¾ cup of corn sugar.

Partial Mash Porter

5 gallon; OG = 1.048; FG = 1.011; IBU = 44; ABV = 4.8%

What a dark, sweet brew this is! Note the 12 oz. of molasses in this recipe. Porter is a brew that you can throw everything (including the kitchen sink!) into, and it will still be good. Other ingredients you might include in this recipe are chocolate, coffee, licorice, juniper berries, ginger — even fresh or dried chili peppers. In Charlie Papazian's book, *The Complete Joy of Home Brewing*, he has a recipe along these lines that he calls "Goat Scrotum Ale." Go ahead and experiment a little.

Ingredients:

1 lb. pale malt (2 row)

1 lb. Munich malt

1 lb. crystal malt (40 °L)

½ lb. chocolate malt

½ lb. black patent malt

¼ lb. roasted barley (500 °L)

½ lb. Briess Golden Light DME

3 ³⁄₁₀ lbs. Briess Golden Light LME (late addition)

12 fl. oz. (355 ml) molasses (15 minutes)

1 tsp. Irish moss (15 minutes)

1 ½ oz. Northern Brewer hops (60 minutes) (9% alpha acids)

¼ oz. Fuggles hops (15 minutes) (5% alpha acids)

Wyeast 1968 (London ESB) or White Labs WLP002 (English Ale)

⅞ cup corn sugar (for priming)

Directions:

1. Heat 5 ½ quarts of water to 169 degrees.

2. Transfer heated water to mash lauter tun.

3. Mash crushed grains at 158 degrees for 30 minutes.

4. Bring ½ gallon of water to boil in a brew pot.

5. Recirculate, run off first wort (a little more than a gallon).

6. Heat 5 ½ qts. of water to 180 degrees in a large saucepan. (This will be your sparge water.)

7. Collect first wort, and transfer it to ¾ gallon of boiling water in your brew pot.

8. Gently add 180-degree sparge water to mash lauter tun.

9. Allow grains in mash lauter tun to rest for five minutes.

10. Recirculate wort in mash lauter tun.

11. Run off second wort, and gently add to brew pot. (You now have about 3 ¼ gallons of wort in the brew pot.)

12. Bring wort to a boil.

13. Add DME and bittering hops to wort.

14. Boil for 60 minutes.

15. After 45 minutes, remove wort from heat.

16. Add Irish moss, molasses, flavoring hops, and LME to wort with 15 minutes left in boil.

17. Return wort to boil.

18. Remove wort for heat after a total boil of 60 minutes

19. Cool wort as quickly as possible to about 80 degrees.

20. Transfer wort to fermenter.

21. Add cool water to bring wort volume to 5 gallons.

22. When wort reaches 72 to 68 degrees, aerate, and pitch yeast.

23. Ferment at 70 degrees for two weeks in primary fermenter.

24. Bottle condition with 7/8 cup of corn sugar.

India Pale Ale

The dry hoppiness of a good pale ale might be an acquired taste, but those that love the hop love this beer. You will, too.

There is a technique in this recipe that will be new to you. You will note that the Saaz hops are listed as first wort hops. This means that these hops are added to the brew pot when you begin to draw off the first wort from the mash lauter tun.

Another new term that you will see in this recipe is "knockout." This refers to the time when you remove the wort from the heat after the boil.

5 gallons; OG = 1.073 FG = 1.017; IBU = 100; ABV = 8%

Ingredients:

2 lbs. pale malt (2 row)

½ lb. crystal malt 60L

6 oz. Weyermann CaraHell

2 oz. Briess Special Roast

7 lbs Briess Pilsen Light DME

1 oz. Saaz hops (first wort hops) (5% alpha acids)

1 ½ oz. Chinook hops (90 minutes) (12% alpha acids)

1 oz. Irish moss (15 minutes)

1 ⅘ oz. Northern Brewer hops (five minutes) (9% alpha acids)

1 ⅘ oz. Cascade hops (five minutes after knockout) (6% alpha acids)

1 ½ oz. Cascade hops (dry hop) (6% alpha acids)

Wyeast American Ale (1056)

¾ cup corn sugar (priming)

Directions:

1. Heat 5 ½ quarts of water to 165 degrees.

2. Transfer heated water to mash lauter tun.

3. Mash crushed grains at 155 degrees for 60 minutes.

4. Bring ¾ gallon of water to boil in a brew pot.

5. Recirculate, run off first wort (a little more than a gallon).

6. Heat 5 ½ qts. of water to 180 degrees in a large saucepan. (This will be your sparge water.)

7. Collect first wort, and transfer it to ¾ gallon of boiling water in your brew pot.

8. Add 1 oz. Saaz hops to first wort in brew pot.

9. Gently add 180-degree sparge water to mash lauter tun.

10. Allow grains in mash lauter tun to rest for five minutes.

11. Recirculate wort in mash lauter tun.

12. Run off second wort, and gently add to brew pot. (You now have about 3 ¼ gallons of wort in the brew pot.)

13. Bring wort to a boil.

14. Add DME and bittering hops to wort.

15. Boil for 90 minutes.

16. After 75 minutes, add Irish moss.

17. Add Aroma hops (1 ⅘ oz. Northern Brewer hops) to wort with five minutes remaining in boil.

18. Remove wort from heat (knockout) after a total boil of 90 minutes.

19. Allow to wort to rest five minutes.

20. Add 1 ⅘ oz. Cascade hops.

21. Cool wort as quickly as possible to about 80 degrees.

22. Transfer wort to fermenter.

23. Add cool water to bring wort volume to 5 gallons.

24. When wort reaches 72 to 68 degrees, aerate, and pitch yeast.

25. Ferment at 70 degrees for one week in primary fermenter.

26. Transfer to secondary fermenter.

27. Add 1 ½ oz. Cascade hops (dry hop).

28. Allow two weeks in secondary fermenter.

29. Bottle condition with ¾ cup of corn sugar.

Partial Mash Irish Red Ale

5 gallons; OG = 1.060; FG = 1.015; IBU = 28; ABV = 5.8%

Ingredients:

2 ½ lbs. light dried malt extract

5 ½ lbs. light dried malt extract (late addition)

6 ½ oz. 2-row pale ale malt

1 lb. crystal malt (40°L)

6 oz. crystal malt (60°L)

2 oz. crystal malt (90°L)

1 ½ oz. roasted barley (300°L)

1 oz. Challenger hops (60 minutes) (7% alpha acids)

½ oz. Kent Goldings hops (30 minutes) (5% alpha acids)

¼ oz. Fuggles hops (five minutes)

1 tsp. Irish moss

Wyeast 1084 (Irish ale) or White Labs WLP004 (Irish ale) yeast

¾ cup corn sugar (for priming)

Directions:

1. Heat 3 quarts of water to 161 degrees.

2. Transfer heated water to mash lauter tun.

3. Mash crushed grains at 150 degrees for 45 minutes.

4. Bring 2 gallons of water to boil in a brew pot.

5. Recirculate, run off first wort (a little more than a gallon).

6. Heat 1 ½ qts. of water to 170 degrees in a large saucepan. (This will be your sparge water.)

7. Collect first wort, and transfer it to 2 gallons of boiling water in your brew pot.

8. Gently add 170-degree sparge water to mash lauter tun.

9. Allow grains in mash lauter tun to rest for five minutes.

10. Recirculate wort in mash lauter tun.

11. Run off second wort, and gently add to brew pot. (You now have about 3 gallons of wort in the brew pot.).

12. Bring wort to a boil.

13. Add 2 ½ lbs DME and Challenger (bittering) hops to wort.

14. Boil for 60 minutes.

15. After 30 minutes, add ½ oz. Kent Goldings hops.

16. After 45 minutes, remove wort from heat.

17. Add Irish moss and 5 ½ lbs DME to wort with 15 minutes left in boil.

18. Return wort to boil.

19. Add Fuggles (aroma) hops to wort with five minutes remaining in boil.

20. Remove wort for heat after a total boil of 60 minutes.

21. Cool wort as quickly as possible to about 80 degrees.

22. Transfer wort to fermenter.

23. Add cool water to bring wort volume to 5 gallons.

24. When wort reaches 72 to 68 degrees, aerate, and pitch yeast.

25. Ferment at 70 degrees for two weeks in primary fermenter.

26. Transfer to secondary fermenter for two weeks.

27. Bottle condition with ¾ cup of corn sugar

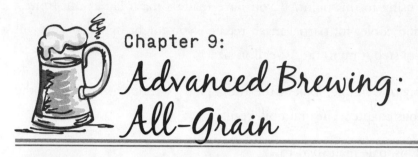

Chapter 9:
Advanced Brewing: All-Grain

All-grain brewing is the pinnacle of the home brewing experience. The reason many brewers make the transition from extract brewing, to partial mash brewing, and on to all-grain brewing is the control it gives you over the entire process. The only way that you can have more control is to grow your own ingredients, and even then, due to climate and environment, you still would not have the level of control that the modern home brewer has with the availability of ingredients at local home-brew stores and online retailers.

If you have brewed a couple of partial mash recipes and feel you understand the process, you are probably ready to try an all-grain beer. The difference in the techniques comes down to a difference, or differences, in volume. Because you will be mashing a larger amount of grain for a typical 5-gallon batch to make up for the absence of malt extract, you will be required to use more water and a larger brew pot than you have been using to this point. If you have made a mash lauter tun from a 5-gallon cooler for partial mash recipes, you might find that you will need to step it up to the 10-gallon size.

By way of example, look at the India pale ale recipe at the end of the previous chapter. The grain bill reads:

2 lbs. pale malt (two-row)

½ lb. crystal malt (60°L)

6 oz. Weyermann CaraHell

2 oz. Briess Special Roast

7 lbs. Briess Pilsen Light DME

 Brew Note: The grain bill is the total list of the grains that are used in any particular beer recipe.

An all-grain recipe of this type might have a grain bill such as:

11 lbs. pale malt (two-row)

½ lb. crystal malt (60°L)

6 oz. Weyermann CaraHell

2 oz. Briess Special Roast

The extract noted in the partial mash recipe is gone, and all of the fermentables will come from mashing the 11 lbs. of pale malt. The total grain bill in this IPA is 12 lbs. A good rule of thumb is that you will mash with 1 quart of water for every pound of grain. That would give your mash 12 lbs. of grain and 3 gallons of water. You will recall that the partial mash recipes employed about 5 ½ quarts of water for the mash.

In the end, you will still be making a 5-gallon batch of beer, so as the procedure continues, things eventually will even out. But in the early stages, the volume of grain and water (hot water) you will be using is considerably different than anything you have done before.

Three basic techniques are associated with all-grain brewing: single-step infusion, step mash (or multi-step infusion), and decoction. These methods are progressively more complex. Each of these techniques will be described here. As you proceed through the following chapters, you will see that these methods of brewing, while offering the opportunity to control every step of the brewing process, are extremely complex and will require a good deal of brewing experience. It is recommended that you seek the assistance and guidance of a home brewer experienced in decoction before you actually attempt it.

All-Grain Equipment

Like many other hobbies, when you get to this level of involvement, the "stuff" factor rises considerably. Home brewing is no exception to this rule. *Brew Your Own* magazine is the "must have" periodical for the home-brew enthusiast. Looking through a recent issue you will see display ads for 10- to 30- gallon stainless steel brew pots, stainless steel two-piece conical fermenters, modular brew stands that will accommodate three tiers of brewing vessels, grain mills, wort chillers, complete brew systems that include two burner propane stoves, brewing software to assist in recipe formulation and mash scheduling, and, as one retailer puts it: "Equipment from Beginner to Insane."

Looking at equipment, you need to decide what you want and what you really need. Look back at the historical recipes given in Chapter 1, and ask yourself if Ben Franklin had a three-tiered modular brewing system. Probably not. If you have made it this far into this book though, you probably want one. Is it a necessity? No. In fact, you can do an all-grain brew using the same equipment you used for the partial mash, but it is much more involved, and you would have to operate in smaller batches and combine them at the end of a long day of brewing. So, to get off on a reasonable path, you will find it necessary to have a 10-gallon mash lauter tun that you can fashion yourself from a 10-gallon plastic, insulated drink dispenser or cooler. You also will require a 35-quart (8 ¾ gallons) stainless steel brew pot. Once you find your footing with this basic equipment, you can go insane and convert your garage into a lagering cooler.

The other equipment you will need to engage in all-grain brewing is what you have already been using to do the partial mashes and extract with grain brews. That is, the smaller pots, thermometers, hydrometers, siphons, tubes, etc.

Your First All-Grain Brew

The best way to get a feel for all-grain brewing is to begin by choosing an all-grain recipe version of a beer you brewed as an extract and as a partial mash. If such a recipe exists, it is an even more educational experience if you still have bottles of that beer in storage so you will be able to taste and compare the final products together.

Considering that advice, the beer that will be used as an explanatory recipe here for all-grain brewing will be porter. You will find an extract porter recipe in Chapter 6 and a recipe for partial mash porter in Chapter 8.

Single-Step Infusion

The process that will be used in this recipe is called single-step infusion mashing. This technique is the easiest to understand at this point because it is near the partial mash technique described in the previous chapters.

To do a single-step infusion mash, you will need the same equipment you used in the partial mash, but to make the same 5-gallon batch of beer, you will need your equipment to be about twice as big. Rather than using that 4 ½-gallon brew pot, you will need one that is about 8 ½ gallons. Rather than using the 5-gallon mash lauter tun you constructed from the insulated drink cooler, you will need to get a 10-gallon insulated drink cooler to construct a larger mash lauter tun.

Although it is not absolutely necessary, you also might want to make or invest in a wort chiller, as the volume of hot wort you will be working with will take longer to cool than the smaller amounts you worked with in the extract and partial mash recipes. The wort chiller will make fast work of cooling off the larger volume of wort. You will recall that the reasons you want a quick chill are to keep the unwanted bacteria from attacking your wort, and you will avoid chill haze by quickly chilling.

The following is an overview of the all-grain single-step infusion mash technique:

1. Determine the amount of water you will need to mash the total amount of grain in your recipe. This water is referred to as your strike water. Remember the rule-of-thumb that you will need one quart of strike water for every pound of grain in your grain bill. For 15 pounds of grain, you will have 15 quarts, or 3 ¾ gallons, of strike water.

2. Determine the amount of sparge water that you will need. This number will float around somewhat depending on your recipe, but you will need at least as much sparge water as strike water and sometimes as much as one and a half times as much sparge water as strike water.

3. Heat the strike water in a large pot. The rule of thumb here is that you will heat the strike water to about 10 to 12 degrees higher than the mash temperature. Example: The porter recipe below instructs you to heat the strike water to 168 degrees for a 156-degree mash temperature.

4. As you are heating the strike water, fill the mash lauter tun with hot water. This water is to warm the inside of the mash lauter tun so

you do not experience too much heat loss as you transfer the strike water and grain to the mash lauter tun.

5. As you are heating the strike water, be heating the sparge water to 170 to 190 degrees.

6. When your strike water hits the target temperature, empty the mash lauter tun of the hot water warming it up, and pour the strike water into the tun.

7. Add the grain to the strike water in the mash lauter tun, and stir it to ensure all the grain is submerged.

8. Cover the mash lauter tun and allow it to rest for ten minutes.

9. Open the mash lauter tun, and take a temperature reading. Adjust the temperature with cold or hot water, depending on the need to get the temperature to your mash target temperature.

10. Place the cover back on the mash lauter tun and allow the mash to rest for the time indicated in the recipe.

11. After you allow the mash to rest for the required time, draw about a quart of wort off through the spigot of your mash lauter tun, and pour it gently back over the resting wort. This quart of wort might be pretty grainy. Repeat this act several times until the runoff is clear of debris. It will not be clear, but it should be relatively free of grain.

12. Once the runoff is free of grain, draw off the contents of the mash lauter tun, and transfer it to a brew pot.

13. Turn the heat on the brew pot to boil.

14. Once you have collected the first wort from the mash lauter tun, add heated sparge water to the grain in the tun. Add enough sparge water so the grain is under about 1 inch of liquid.

15. Draw about a quart of the second wort off through the spigot of your mash lauter tun, and pour it gently back over the resting wort. This quart of wort also might be grainy. Repeat this act several times until the runoff is clear of debris.

16. Collect this second wort and gently add it to the first wort in the brew pot. Add enough wort so you have your target volume (in this case, 5 gallons) plus about ½ gallon.

17. Once your brew pot has reached 5 ½ gallons, take a hydrometer reading of the remaining runoff in the mash lauter tun. If the runoff reads below 1.010, stop adding it to the brew pot. If your runoff is above that number, you can add another quart or two to your brew pot. When you take this hydrometer reading, remember to adjust for wort temperature.

18. Once you have finished transferring wort from the mash lauter tun to your brew pot, allow the wort to come to a rolling boil.

19. Add the hops and other adjunct ingredients according to recipe schedule.

20. Once your boil is complete according to beer recipe, remove the brew pot from the heat, and stir it well.

21. Cover the brew pot, and allow it to rest for ten minutes.

22. After the ten-minute rest, chill the beer as quickly as possible.

23. Transfer the beer to a cleaned and sanitized fermenter, and follow recipe instructions regarding yeast pitch, fermentation, and bottling.

All-Grain Porter

5 gallons; OG = 1.066; FG = 1.021; IBU = 30; ABV = 5.9%

Ingredients:

12 ½ lbs. pale malt (two-row)

1 lb. crystal malt (60°L)

⅔ lb. chocolate malt

⅔ lb. black malt

⅓ lb. roasted barley

(Note: 15.15 lbs. of grain)

Brew Note: Compare this all-grain recipe grain bill to the grain bill/fermentable ingredients of the partial mash porter recipe in Chapter 8:

1 lb. pale malt (two-row)

1 lb. Munich malt

1 lb. crystal malt (40°L)

½ lb. chocolate malt

½ lb. black patent malt

¼ lb. roasted barley (500°L)

½ lb. Briess Golden Light DME

3 ³⁄₁₀ lbs. Briess Golden Light LME (late addition)

and the extract with grain recipe in Chapter 6:

Fermentables:

1 lb. Briess Light dried malt extract

4 ⅔ lbs. Briess Light liquid malt extract (late addition)

Specialty Malts:

2 ⅓ lbs. Bonlander Munich malt

1 ¼ lbs. crystal malt (40°L)

1 ¼ lbs. crystal malt (80°L)

¾ lbs. chocolate malt

¼ lbs. black malt

The extract recipe has a total grain bill of 5.83 lbs., though none of the grains are employed as base fermentables. Bonlander Munich is a base fermentable malt. The grains in the extract recipe are there to offer taste and body. The partial mash recipe has 2 lbs. of grain in the grain bill used as partial fermentables: pale malt and Munich malt. The all-grain recipe has 12.5 lbs. of base malt (pale malt).

2 oz. Willamette (60 minutes)

¾ oz. Willamette (30 minutes)

1 tsp. Irish moss (20 minutes)

¾ oz. Cascade hops (ten minutes)

English Ale (White Labs #WLP002)

¾ cup corn sugar (priming)

Directions:

1.   Heat 3 ¾ gallons of water to 168 degrees.

The mash water level in this recipe is about twice as much as the partial mash recipe. There was not a mash in the extract recipe.

2.   Transfer heated water to mash lauter tun.

3.   Mash crushed grains at 156 degrees for 60 minutes.

4.   Recirculate, run off first wort (a little more than a gallon).

5.   Heat 4 ⅓ gallons of water to 168 degrees in a large pot. (This will be your sparge water.)

6.   Collect first wort, and transfer it to your brew pot.

7.   Gently add 168-degree sparge water to mash lauter tun.

8.   Allow grains in mash lauter tun to rest for five minutes.

9. Recirculate wort in mash lauter tun

10. Run off second wort, and gently add to brew pot. (You now have about 6 ¾ gallons of wort in the brew pot.)

You should expect to boil off about ¾ gallon during the boil and about a ¾-gallon trub loss, which is the excess wort left when transferring from the brew pot to the fermenter. This will leave you with a volume of 5 ¼ gallons.

11. Bring wort to a boil.

12. Add bittering hops to wort.

13. Boil for 60 minutes, following hop schedule as indicated in ingredient list.

14. Remove wort for heat after a total boil of 60 minutes.

15. Cool wort as quickly as possible to about 80 degrees.

16. Transfer wort to fermenter.

17. When wort reaches 68 degrees, aerate, and pitch yeast.

18. Ferment at 65 to 68 degrees for two weeks in primary fermenter.

19. Bottle condition with ¾ cup of corn sugar.

You can see that by comparing partial mash brews to all-grain brews that they are much the same except for volume needed to make 5 gallons of beer. You will need a larger brew pot and a larger mash lauter tun, and a wort chiller comes in handy to chill the larger volume of wort quickly.

The brewing process described above is the simplest procedure for all-grain brewing. This procedure is the next advancement from the partial mash procedure described in the preceding chapter, and it is a logical step to take before learning the more advanced all-grain techniques.

The Step Mash

If you have arrived at this stage of your brewing exploration and you still want to learn and experience more about the art, craft, and science of brewing beer, you are about to take a huge leap forward. The step mash (or multi-step or step infusion) technique of all-grain brewing is perfect for those of you who love(d) chemistry and really want to know how and why these processes work the way they do.

Simply put, the step mash process involves holding your wort at specific temperatures for specific periods for specific purposes. This process is most often used on under-modified malted barley.

You will recall from Chapter 3 that modification is the complex stage of the grain development as the individual grain goes from seed to growing plant. Modification describes the degree to which the protein and starches of the grain have been broken down. A grain is considered fully modified when the embryonic barley plant, or acrospire, is about three-fourths the length of the grain. The acrospire is the scientific name for the first shoot that develops from a germinating seed. An under-modified malt is a grain in which the acrospire has appeared, but it is only about half the length of the grain. This means that a more complex process needs to be undertaken by the brewer to use these malts. Examples of under-modified malts are:

Budvar Under-Modified Pale Moravia — This malt needs to be mashed using multiple temperatures.

Spitz Malz — Meussdoerffer Spitz is an under-modified malt that is known to enhance the beer's color and improve its head retention.

Step mashing also is used to control the development of the natural yeast nutrients in the grain, to increase the availability of the grain's starches for conversion into fermentable sugars, and to control protein haze (or chill haze).

The "steps" in this step mash are referred to as rests. In this process, the temperature of the mash is increased by the addition of warmer and warmer strike water to control enzymatic actions of the grain slowly and more accurately specific.

It is conceivable that you could do as many as six or seven rests during the course of a mash with each rest achieving a specific purpose, but this is extreme, even for an experienced brewing enthusiast.

Mash schedules are much like hops schedules in that they will vary from beer to beer. Where hop schedules are designed to influence the IBU, flavor, and aroma of a particular beer, mash schedules are designed to influence the body of the beer. The body of a beer generally is identified as light, medium, or full. Mouthfeel is another word that relates to body. It describes how the beer feels in your mouth: light, medium, or full. The elements that give the beer this feeling are the residual proteins and sugars, or dextrins. The rests in the step mashing process control these elements.

Home brewers today will consider as many as four steps if they engage in this step mash technique. The way each step is handled is determined by the body they seek in their brew.

Step One — Mash In: This first step often is passed over, but it does serve a purpose. This first step would be the same for all beers and is referred to as mash-in or doughing-in. Though all brews will mash in whether you are doing a partial mash or a single-step infusion mash, the mash-in stage of this step mash process can hold the wort at 105 degrees for 20 minutes. This rest gives the grain and their starches adequate time to soak up the strike water.

Step Two — Protein Rest: The protein rest is used, generally, to improve beer clarity. The ideal protein rest temperature for all beers is 122 degrees for 30 minutes. If you have begun your step mash at 105 degrees, raise the temperature of your mash to 122 degrees, and hold it there for 30 minutes. If you did not employ the step one rest, you can just begin your mash at 122 degrees, and hold it there for 30 minutes.

Step Three — Saccharification Rest: This is the rest when the enzymes in the grain convert the starches into fermentable sugars. Knowing that the body of the beer is related to the sugars present, this rest will most effect the beer's mouthfeel. This rest is slightly different depending on the body you seek. This is also a rest where precision of temperature is key.

Brew Note: A simple test used to check on the conversion of starch into fermentable sugar is the iodine test. Draw a couple of drops of wort from your mash lauter tun with a cleaned and sanitized eyedropper, and put the wort on a clean white dish or plate. Make sure there are no solids in your wort. Place a drop of iodine on the wort. The liquid will change color. Purple indicates there is still starch in the wort that needs to be converted; total mash saccharification will be noted when there is no change in the yellow color of iodine.

For light-bodied beer, increase the temperature from the protein rest temperature of 122 degrees to 150 degrees and hold it there for 25 minutes. After 20 minutes, do an iodine test on the wort. If the iodine does not change (indicated total saccharification), you can proceed to the next step. If the iodine indicates that total saccharification has not occurred, allow the mash to rest another five to ten minutes and perform another iodine test.

For medium-bodied beer, the saccharification rest will be at 150 degrees for ten minutes followed by an increase in temperature to 158 degrees for 20 minutes. After 20 minutes at 158 degrees, do an iodine test on the wort. If the iodine does not change (indicated total saccharification), you can proceed to the next step. If the iodine indicates total saccharification has not occurred, allow the mash to rest another five to ten minutes and perform another iodine test.

For a full-bodied beer the saccharification rest will be at 158 degrees for 20 minutes. After 20 minutes at 158 degrees, do an iodine test on the wort. If the iodine does not change (indicated total saccharification), you can proceed to the next step. If the iodine indicates total saccharification has not occurred, allow the mash to rest another ten minutes and perform another iodine test.

Step Four — Mash out: The mash out is the action you take to halt the enzymatic activity of the wort. Remember in the partial mash technique, this was accomplished by adding the wort to boiling water in your brew tank. In this step mash technique, you will raise the temperature of the mash to 168 to 170 degrees. Once the mash has reached this target temperature, you will hold it there for ten minutes. This step is the same for all bodies of beer.

Step Five: What you do at this point will be determined by the equipment you have been using. You might have noticed along the steps in this process that if you are considering doing a step mash with a mash lauter tun that has been converted from an insulated drink cooler, you have added a great deal of water to increase the temperature in steps as you have. This is not an impossible task, but it is not the most efficient way to go about this process. If you have gotten to this point in your beer-making expertise, you probably already have seen the wisdom of using separate mash tuns and lauter tuns.

Step five involves transferring the mash out of the mash tun and into the lauter tun where the sparging will take place. Slowly sparge the grain with sparge water heated to about 168 degrees. This process will take about an hour. Collect the wort as you sparge and transfer to a brew pot.

The step mash is complete, and you continue with your wort in the same manner you did with the single-step infusion mash.

Irish Red Ale

5 gallons; OG = 1.054 measured;

FG = 1.012 measured; IBU = 28; ABV = 5.5%

Here is a recipe for Irish red ale described in the step mash process. You can make this recipe using the single-step infusion process, as well by employing the same grain bill and following the mash procedure described in the single-step process described earlier in this chapter.

Irish red ale is a well-balanced brew, though this recipe has a slightly higher hop character than the standard IRA.

Ingredients:

Grain bill:

   9 ½ lbs. pale malt (two-row)

   1 lb. Vienna malt

   1 lb. crystal malt (60°L)

   ¼ lb. rye malt

   ⅛ lb. chocolate malt

Total grain bill of 11.875 lbs.

Hops and adjunct schedule:

   ½ oz. Chinook (55 minutes) (11% alpha acids)

½ oz. Fuggles (30 minutes) (4.3% alpha acids)

1 tsp. Irish Moss (ten minutes)

¼ oz. East Kent Goldings (5 minutes) (5% alpha acids)

1 Tbsp. Gypsum (Calcium Sulfate) in sparge water

Yeast

Wyeast British Ale (1098)

Directions:

1. Heat 4 ¼ gallons of water to 105 degrees in a mash tun.

The strike water level in this recipe is 1 ½ quarts for each pound of grain. The grain bill is 11.875 lbs. x 1.5 = 17.8125 qts. = 4.45 gals. Round down to 4.25 gallons.

2. Add grains to heated mash tun, and hold for 20 minutes (mash-in).

3. Raise mash temperature to 122 degrees.

4. Mash crushed grains at 122 degrees for 30 minutes (protein rest).

5. Raise mash temperature to 150 degrees.

6. Mash crushed grains at 150 degrees for ten minutes (saccharification rest).

7. Heat 4.25 gallons of sparge water to 170 degrees.

8. Add gypsum to sparge water.

Brew Note: Gypsum (calcium sulfate) is used here in the sparge water to accentuate the bitterness of the hops. You could liken it to adding a little salt to your food to accentuate the flavor.

9. Raise mash temperature to 158 degrees.

10. Mash crushed grains at 158 degrees for 20 minutes (saccharification rest).

11. Raise mash temperature to 168 degrees.

12. Mash crushed grains at 168 degrees for 15 minutes (mash-out).

13. Transfer contents of mash tun to lauter tun.

14. Recirculate, run off first wort (a little more than a gallon).

15. Collect first wort, and transfer it to your brew pot.

16. Gently add 170-degree sparge water to mash lauter tun.

17. Allow grains in mash lauter tun to rest for five minutes

18. Recirculate wort in mash lauter tun.

19. Run off second wort, and gently add to brew pot. (You now have about 6 ¾ gallons of wort in the brew pot)

You should expect to boil off about ¾ gallon during the boil and about a ¾-gallon trub loss. This will leave you with a volume of 5 ¼ gallons.

20. Bring wort to a boil.

21. Boil for a total of 60 minutes following hop schedule as indicated in ingredient list.

22. Remove wort for heat after a total boil of 60 minutes.

23. Cool wort as quickly as possible to about 80 degrees.

24. Transfer wort to fermenter.

25. When wort reaches 68 degrees, aerate, and pitch yeast.

26. Ferment at 65 to 68 degrees for two weeks in primary fermenter.

27. Bottle condition with ¾ cup of corn sugar.

28. Allow a minimum of three weeks to condition in the bottle.

If you are still brewing with that converted drink-dispensing cooler mash lauter tun, you might have to rethink your setup if you plan to do a step mash. As you might have figured out reading this recipe for Irish red ale, it is a complicated matter to add just the right amount of water at just the right temperature to hit that step target. If you are at this stage of your brewing experience, you probably are using a separate mash tun, and if you are not, you should be.

Decoction

To decoct is to extract by boiling. Decoction mashing is a way of extracting starches from a portion of the grain. The method was originated in a time before the use of the thermometer when strict temperature control was not as easy as it is today. Decoction mashing remains a part of an advanced brewing repertoire because of the unique quality it gives the resulting brew.

Decoction, like infusion, can occur in a single step or in multiple steps, depending on the beer recipe and the brewer's experience. To do a decoction mash, you will need to have an additional brew pot at your disposal because decoction calls for boiling a portion of the grain while continuing to mash the rest of the grain. In the step mash, you used hot water to increase the mash temperature. In decoction mashing, you will use the boiled mash to increase the temperature of the rest of the batch.

The basic premise of decoction mashing is to remove a portion (usually 30 to 40 percent) of the mash out of the mash tun and transfer it to a brew pot where you will boil it for a specific amount of time, depending on the goal of the specific step of the mash. After boiling, the mixture is returned to the mash tun, and you continue with your mash schedule.

The following descriptions will explain single, double, and triple decoction mash schedules. After describing these schedules, there is a recipe for a pilsner that will employ a triple decoction mash schedule. The reason that a brewer may choose to employ a double decoction rather than a single decoction is to bring out a specific quality in the beer that is being brewed. A double decoction may, for example, bring out the flavor of a particular grain that the brewer would like to highlight in the beer.

The employment of a single, double, or triple decoction is up to the brewer, their ability to do it based on their skill and equipment, and, of course, their taste. While these methods are by no means necessary, the craft brew enthusiast will enjoy trying it.

Brew Note: A couple of new terms will be used from here on to describe water and grain. "Liquor" will be used to refer to the water used in the mash process. "Grist" is the word used to describe the grain used to make the beer. The liquor and grist are mashed to make the wort.

Single decoction mash schedule

1. Heat liquor (water) to about 110 degrees. You want to start with about three times as much liquor as grist.

2. Stir the grist into the liquor. Do this by rapidly stirring the liquor as you add the grist. Stir well until all of the grist has been incorporated into the liquor. The target temperature you are aiming for is 100 degrees. The 110-degree liquor will drop slightly when you add the cooler grist. This stage is the mash-in or dough-in stage.

3. Raise the mash temperature slowly (about 2 degrees a minute) to 122 degrees. This is the temperature of the protein rest.

4. Cover the pot and hold at 122 degrees for a 20-minute protein rest.

Brew Note: This protein rest will be longer if you are brewing a wheat beer using this decoction mash technique. It takes a longer time to break down the protein in wheat.

5. Remove 30 to 40 percent of the liquor and grist from the mash tun, and transfer it to a brew pot. You will remove this mash at a ratio of about two parts liquor to one part grist.

6. Cover the first pot.

7. Raise the temperature of the removed mash to 158 degrees.

8. Hold removed mash at 158 degrees for 20 minutes.

9. Raise removed mash to boil.

10. Boil removed mash for 20 minutes.

11. Return removed mash to mash tun.

12. Allow mash to rest for 20 minutes.

13. Increase heat of mash tun to 158 degrees.

14. Allow mash to rest for 20 minutes.

15. Increase heat of mash tun to 170 degrees for ten minutes.

16. Transfer mash to lauter tun.

17. Sparge with 168-degree water.

18. The decoction is complete, and you continue with your wort in the same manner you did with the single-step infusion mash.

Double decoction mash schedule

1. Heat liquor (water) to about 110 degrees. You want to start with about three times as much liquor as grist.

2. Stir the grist into the liquor. Stir well until all of the grist has been incorporated into the liquor. The target temperature you are

aiming at is 100 degrees. The 110-degree liquor will drop slightly when you add the cooler grist.

3. Raise the mash temperature slowly (about 2 degrees a minute) to 122 degrees. This is the temperature of the protein rest.

4. Cover the pot, and hold at 122 degrees for a 20-minute protein rest.

5. Remove 30 to 40 percent of the liquor and grist from the mash tun, and transfer it to a brew pot. You will remove this mash at a ratio of about two parts liquor to one part grist.

6. Cover the first pot.

7. Raise the temperature of the removed mash to 150 degrees.

8. Hold removed mash at 150 degrees for 20 minutes.

9. Raise removed mash to boil.

10. Boil removed mash for 15 minutes.

11. Return removed mash to mash tun very slowly over a ten-minute period.

12. Allow mash to rest for 20 minutes. This mash should be about 148 degrees.

13. Remove 30 to 40 percent of the liquor and grist from the mash tun, and transfer it to a brew pot.

14. Cover the first pot.

15. Raise the temperature of the removed mash to 150 degrees.

16. Hold removed mash at 150 degrees for 20 minutes.

17. Raise removed mash to boil.

18. Boil removed mash for 15 minutes.

19. Return removed mash to mash tun slowly over a ten-minute period.

20. Allow mash to rest for 20 minutes. This mash should be about 148 degrees.

21. Raise mash temperature to 158 degrees

22. Hold mash at 158 degrees for 15 minutes

23. Perform an iodine test. If iodine does not change color, continue to next step. If iodine changes color, allow to rest for another five to ten minutes. Do another iodine test. When iodine does not change color, you may continue.

24. Raise mash temperature to 170 degrees.

25. Hold mash temperature at 170 degrees for ten minutes.

26. Transfer mash to lauter tun.

27. Sparge with 168-degree water.

28. The decoction is complete, and you continue with your wort in the same manner you did with the single-step infusion mash.

Triple decoction mash schedule

1. Heat liquor (water) to about 100 degrees. You want to start with about three times as much liquor as grist.

2. Stir the grist into the liquor. Stir well until all of the grist has been incorporated into the liquor. The target temperature you are aiming at is 95 degrees. The 100-degree liquor will drop slightly when you add the cooler grist.

3. Hold mash at 95 degrees for 30 minutes.

4. Remove 30 to 40 percent of the liquor and grist from the mash tun, and transfer it to a brew pot. You will remove this mash at a ratio of about two parts liquor to one part grist.

5. Cover the first pot.

6. Raise the temperature of the removed mash to 150 degrees.

7. Hold removed mash at 150 degrees for 20 minutes.

8. Raise removed mash to boil.

9. Boil removed mash for five minutes.

10. Return removed mash to mash tun very slowly over a ten-minute period.

11. Allow mash to rest for 20 minutes. This mash should be about 148 degrees.

12. Remove 30 to 40 percent of the liquor and grist from the mash tun, and transfer it to a brew pot.

13. Cover the first pot.

14. Raise the temperature of the removed mash to 150 degrees.

15. Hold removed mash at 150 degrees for 20 minutes.

16. Raise removed mash to boil.

17. Boil removed mash for 15 minutes.

18. Return removed mash to mash tun slowly over a ten-minute period.

19. Allow mash to rest for 20 minutes. This mash should be about 148 degrees.

20. Remove 30 to 40 percent of the liquor and grist from the mash tun, and transfer it to a brew pot.

21. Cover the first pot.

22. Raise the temperature of the removed mash to 150 degrees.

23. Hold removed mash at 150 degrees for 20 minutes.

24. Raise removed mash to boil.

25. Boil removed mash for 30 minutes.

26. Return removed mash to mash tun very slowly over a ten-minute period.

27. Allow mash to rest for 20 minutes. This mash should be about 148 degrees.

28. Raise mash temperature to 158 degrees.

29. Hold mash at 158 degrees for 15 minutes.

30. Perform an iodine test. If iodine does not change color, continue to next step. If iodine changes color, allow to rest for another five to ten minutes. Do another iodine test. When iodine does not change color, you may continue.

31. Raise mash temperature to 170 degrees.

32. Hold mash temperature at 170 degrees for ten minutes.

33. Transfer mash to lauter tun.

34. Sparge with 168-degree water.

35. The decoction is complete, and you continue with your wort in the same manner you did with the single-step infusion mash.

The schedules noted above are rule-of-thumb schedules that might change depending on the specific nature of the recipe you employ. They can be used in just about any decoction recipe, but again, the style of beer you brew might call for slight differences in temperature or rest time from step to step.

As with the descriptions of other brew techniques, a specific recipe will be used here to demonstrate the use of decoction in all-grain brewing. This particular recipe will employ a triple decoction mash.

Bohemian Pilsner

5 gallons; OG = 1.054; FG = 1.013; IBU = 40; ABV = 5.3%

Ingredients:

Grain bill:

10 lbs. German two-row Pilsner malt

¼ lb. German crystal malt (2 ½ L)

¼ lb. German Munich malt

Hops:

3 oz. Czech Saaz (3.5% alpha acid) (60 minutes)

1 oz. Czech Saaz (3.5% alpha acid) (20 minutes)

1 tsp. Irish moss (ten minutes)

1 oz. Czech Saaz (3.5% alpha acid) (five minutes)

½ oz. Czech Saaz (3.5% alpha acid) (dry hop)

Yeast:

Wyeast 2278 Czech Pils

¾ cup corn sugar (priming)

Directions:

1. Heat liquor (water) to about 130 degrees. You want to start with about three times as much liquor as grist to be used.

2. Stir the grist into the liquor. Do this by rapidly stirring the liquor as you add the grist. Stir well until all of the grist has been incorporated into the liquor. The target temperature you are aiming at is 122 degrees. The 130-degree liquor will drop slightly when you add the cooler grist. This stage is the mash-in or dough-in stage.

3. Hold mash at 122 degrees for 25 minutes.

4. Remove 30 to 40 percent of the liquor and grist from the mash tun, and transfer it to a brew pot. You will remove this mash at a ratio of about two parts liquor to one part grist.

5. Cover the first pot.

6. Raise the temperature of the removed mash to 150 degrees.

7. Hold removed mash at 150 degrees for 20 minutes.

8. Raise removed mash to boil.

9. As soon as the mash reaches a boil, remove it from the heat.

10. Return removed mash to mash tun slowly over a ten-minute period.

11. Allow mash to rest for 20 minutes. This mash should be about 145 degrees.

12. Remove 30 to 40 percent of the liquor and grist from the mash tun, and transfer it to a brew pot.

13. Cover the first pot.

14. Raise the temperature of the removed mash to 150 degrees.

15. Hold removed mash at 150 degrees for 20 minutes.

16. Raise removed mash to boil.

17. As soon as the mash reaches a boil, remove it from the heat.

18. Return removed mash to mash tun slowly over a ten-minute period.

19. Allow mash to rest for one hour. This mash should be about 152 degrees.

20. Remove 30 to 40 percent of the liquor and grist from the mash tun, and transfer it to a brew pot.

21. Cover the first pot.

22. Raise the temperature of the removed mash to 150 degrees.

23. Hold removed mash at 150 degrees for 20 minutes.

24. Raise removed mash to boil.

25. As soon as the mash reaches a boil, remove it from the heat.

26. Return removed mash to mash tun slowly over a ten-minute period.

27. Allow mash to rest for 20 minutes. This mash should be about 168 degrees.

28. Hold mash at 168 degrees for 15 minutes.

29. Heat 4 ⅓ gallons of water to 168 degrees in a large pot. (This will be your sparge water.)

30. Perform an iodine test. If iodine does not change color, continue to next step. If iodine changes color, allow to rest for another five to ten minutes. Do another iodine test. When iodine does not change color, you may continue.

31. Raise mash temperature to 170 degrees.

32. Hold mash temperature at 170 degrees for ten minutes.

33. Transfer mash to lauter tun.

34. Sparge with 168-degree water.

35. Collect first wort, and transfer it to your brew pot.

36. Gently add 168-degree sparge water to mash lauter tun.

37. Allow grains in mash lauter tun to rest for five minutes.

38. Recirculate wort in mash lauter tun.

39. Run off second wort, and gently add to brew pot. (You now have about 6 ¾ gallons of wort in the brew pot.)

You should expect to boil off about ¾ gallon during the boil and about a ¾-gallon trub loss. This will leave you with a volume of 5 ¼ gallons.

40. Bring wort to a boil.

41. Add 3 oz. Czech Saaz hops to wort.

42. Boil for 60 minutes, following hop schedule as indicated in ingredient list.

43. Remove wort for heat after a total boil of 60 minutes.

44. Cool wort as quickly as possible to about 80 degrees.

45. Transfer wort to fermenter.

46. When wort reaches 56 degrees, aerate, and pitch yeast.

47. Ferment at 50 to 56 degrees for two weeks in primary fermenter.

48. Bottle condition with ¾ cup of corn sugar.

49. Allow beer to carbonate at about 70 degrees for at least three weeks.

50. Store carbonated beer in a cool place.

This Bohemian Pilsner recipe can be made using only one decoction by doing a mash-out after step 11. To do this, you will raise the mash temperature to 168 through 170 degrees and allow the mash to rest at that temperature for about 15 minutes. From that point on, you will pick up the recipe instructions at step 33. Do not forget to heat your sparge water as the mash is doing its final rest.

You also may employ the ingredients of this recipe in any of the all-grain brewing techniques described in the preceding chapters. As with any of the recipes in this book, you can adjust them to your own tastes by changing ingredients and experimenting with adjunct ingredients. You know what you like.

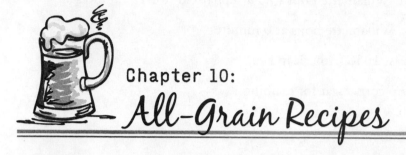

Chapter 10:
All-Grain Recipes

The recipes shown here are all written as single-infusion mash recipes. Any of these all-grain recipes can be brewed as step-mashes or decoctions, as well.

American Amber Ale

5 gallons; OG = 1.052; FG = 1.012: ABV = 5%; 23 IBUs

Ingredients:

8 lbs. two-row pale malt

1 lb. carapils or dextrin-type malt

½ lb. crystal malt (80°L)

¼ lb. crystal malt (120°L)

¼ lb. chocolate malt

¼ oz. Centennial hops (2.75% alpha acid) for 90 minutes

¾ oz. Willamette hops (3.5% alpha acid) for 15 minutes

1 oz. Willamette hops at 0 minutes

Wyeast 1056 (American ale)

⅔ cup corn sugar for priming

Directions:

1. Heat 3 ¼ gallons of water to 164 degrees.

2. Transfer heated water to mash lauter tun.

3. Mash crushed grains at 150 degrees for 60 minutes.

4. Recirculate, run off first wort (a little more than a gallon).

5. Heat 3 ¼ gallons of water to 168 degrees in a large pot. (This will be your sparge water.)

6. Collect first wort, and transfer it to your brew pot.

7. Gently add 168-degree sparge water to mash lauter tun.

8. Allow grains in mash lauter tun to rest for five minutes.

9. Recirculate wort in mash lauter tun.

10. Run off second wort, and gently add to brew pot. (You now have about 5 ¾ gallons of wort in the brew pot.)

11. Bring wort to a boil.

12. Add Centennial hops to wort.

13. Boil for 90 minutes, following hop schedule as indicated in ingredient list.

14. Remove wort for heat after a total boil of 90 minutes.

15. Cool wort as quickly as possible to about 70 degrees.

16. Transfer wort to fermenter.

17. When wort reaches 70 degrees, aerate, and pitch yeast.

18. Ferment at 65 to 70 degrees for one week in primary fermenter.

19. Rack to secondary fermenter for one week.

20. Bottle condition with ¾ cup of corn sugar.

21. Allow two weeks to carbonate.

California Common All-Grain

5.0 gallons; OG = 1.054; FG = 1.012; ABV = 5.6%; 32 IBU

Ingredients:

8 ½ lbs. American two-row pale

1 ½ lbs. American crystal (60°L)

1 oz. Northern Brewer (8% alpha acid) for 60 minutes

½ oz. Northern Brewer (8% alpha acid) for 15 minutes

1 tsp. Irish moss for 15 minutes

½ oz. Northern Brewer (8% alpha acid) for five minutes

Wyeast California Lager (2112)

Directions:

1. Heat 3 ¼ gallons of water to 162 degrees.

2. Transfer heated water to mash lauter tun.

3. Mash crushed grains at 154 degrees for 75 minutes.

4. Recirculate, run off first wort (a little more than a gallon).

5. Heat 3 ¼ gallons of water to 168 degrees in a large pot. (This will be your sparge water.)

6. Collect first wort, and transfer it to your brew pot.

7. Gently add 168-degree sparge water to mash lauter tun.

8. Allow grains in mash lauter tun to rest for five minutes.

9. Recirculate wort in mash lauter tun.

10. Run off second wort, and gently add to brew pot. (You now have about 5 ¾ gallons of wort in the brew pot.)

11. Bring wort to a boil.

12. Add Northern Brewer hops to wort.

13. Boil for 60 minutes following hop schedule as indicated in ingredient list.

14. Remove wort for heat after a total boil of 60 minutes.

15. Cool wort as quickly as possible to about 70 degrees.

16. Transfer wort to fermenter.

17. When wort reaches 70 degrees, aerate, and pitch yeast.

18. Ferment at 65 to 70 degrees for one week in primary fermenter.

19. Rack to secondary fermenter for one week.

20. Bottle condition with ¾ cup of corn sugar.

21. Allow two weeks to carbonate.

All-Grain Bock Beer

5 gallons; OG = 1.066 FG = 1.016 IBU = 25, ABV = 6.5%

Ingredients:

6 lbs. two-row lager malt

3 ½ lbs. wheat malt

1 ½ lbs. German crystal malt (40°L)

½ lb. Cara-vienne (20°L)

½ lb. Victory malt (20°L)

½ lb. chocolate malt

1 ¼ oz. Hallertau hops (5.1% alpha acid) 60 minutes

½ oz. Hallertau hops (5.1% alpha acid) 30 minutes

½ oz. Hallertau hops (0.5 oz. at 5.1% alpha acid) 0 minutes

Starter of Wyeast 2206 (Bavarian Lager) or White Labs WLP920 (Old Bavarian Lager)

¾ cup corn sugar (for priming)

Directions:

1. Heat 3 gallons of water to 130 degrees.

2. Transfer heated water to mash lauter tun.

3. Mash crushed grains at 122 degrees for 30 minutes.

4. Add 1 ½ gallons of boiling water to mash. (This will bring mash temperature up to about 155 degrees.)

5. Allow to mash for 45 minutes.

6. Recirculate, run off first wort (a little more than a gallon).

7. Heat 3 ¼ gallons of water to 168 degrees in a large pot. (This will be your sparge water.)

8. Collect first wort, and transfer it to your brew pot.

9. Gently add 168-degree sparge water to mash lauter tun.

10. Allow grains in mash lauter tun to rest for five minutes.

11. Recirculate wort in mash lauter tun.

12. Run off second wort, and gently add to brew pot (you now have about 5 ¾ gallons of wort in the brew pot).

13. Bring wort to a boil.

14. Add Hallertau hops to wort.

15. Boil for 60 minutes, following hop schedule as indicated in ingredient list.

16. Remove wort for heat after a total boil of 60 minutes.

17. Cool wort as quickly as possible to about 55 degrees.

18. Transfer wort to fermenter.

19. Aerate and pitch yeast.

20. Ferment at 55 degrees for two weeks in primary fermenter.

21. Rack to secondary fermenter for two months at about 35 to 40 degrees.

22. Bottle condition with ¾ cup of corn sugar.

23. Allow two weeks to carbonate.

All-Grain Wheat Beer

5 gallons; OG = 1.051; FG = 1.012; IBU = 21; ABV = 5.1%

Ingredients:

5 ½ lbs. wheat malt

4 ½ lbs. pale malt (two-row)

8 oz. rice hulls

1 oz. Cascade hops (5% alpha acid)

White Labs WLP320 (American Hefeweizen) yeast or Wyeast 1010 American Wheat

Directions:

1. Heat 3 ¼ gallons of water to 161 degrees.

2. Transfer heated water to mash lauter tun.

3. Mash crushed grains at 150 degrees for 60 minutes.

4. Recirculate, run off first wort (a little more than a gallon).

5. Heat 3 ¼ gallons of water to 180 degrees in a large pot. (This will be your sparge water.)

6. Collect first wort, and transfer it to your brew pot.

7. Gently add 180-degree sparge water to mash lauter tun.

8. Allow grains in mash lauter tun to rest for five minutes.

9. Recirculate wort in mash lauter tun.

10. Run off second wort, and gently add to brew pot. (You now have about 5 ¾ gallons of wort in the brew pot.)

11. Bring wort to a boil.

12. Add Cascade hops to wort.

13. Boil for 60 minutes.

14. Remove wort for heat after a total boil of 60 minutes.

15. Cool wort as quickly as possible to about 70 degrees.

16. Transfer wort to fermenter.

17. When wort reaches 70 degrees, aerate, and pitch yeast.

18. Ferment at 65 to 70 degrees for two weeks in primary fermenter.

19. Bottle condition with ¾ cup of corn sugar.

20. Allow two weeks to carbonate.

All-Grain India Pale Ale

5 gallons; OG = 1.065; FG = 1.015; IBU = 40; ABV = 6.5%

Ingredients:

11 ¼ lbs. pale malt (two-row)

1 lb. Cara-Pils/Dextrine

1 lb. crystal malt (80°L)

⅓ oz. Chinook (10.50% alpha acid) 90 minutes

⅓ oz. Northern Brewer (8.70% alpha acid) 90 minutes

¼ oz. Cascade (5.70% alpha acid) 90 minutes

¾ oz. Centennial (12.00% alpha acid) 20 minutes

1 oz. Centennial (12.00% alpha acid) Dry hop to secondary fermenter

½ tsp. Irish Moss (Boil ten minutes)

London Ale (Wyeast Labs #1028)

¾ cup corn sugar (priming)

Directions:

1. Heat 4 gallons of water to 164 degrees.

2. Transfer heated water to mash lauter tun.

3. Mash crushed grains at 150 degrees for 60 minutes.

4. Recirculate, run off first wort (a little more than a gallon).

5. Heat 3 ¾ gallons of water to 168 degrees in a large pot. (This will be your sparge water.)

6. Collect first wort, and transfer it to your brew pot.

7. Gently add 168-degree sparge water to mash lauter tun.

8. Allow grains in mash lauter tun to rest for five minutes.

9. Recirculate wort in mash lauter tun.

10. Run off second wort, and gently add to brew pot. (You now have about 5 ¾ gallons of wort in the brew pot.)

11. Bring wort to a boil.

12. Add hops and Irish moss according to hop schedule to wort.

13. Boil for 90 minutes, following hop schedule as indicated in ingredient list.

14. Remove wort for heat after a total boil of 90 minutes.

15. Cool wort as quickly as possible to about 70 degrees.

16. Transfer wort to fermenter.

17. When wort reaches 70 degrees, aerate, and pitch yeast.

18. Ferment at 65 to 70 degrees for one week in primary fermenter.

19. Rack to secondary fermenter for one week.

20. Bottle condition with ¾ cup of corn sugar.

21. Allow two weeks to carbonate.

All Grain ESB

5 gallons; OG = 1.052; FG = 1.013; IBU = 41; ABV = 5.7%

Ingredients:

11 ⅔ lbs. pale malt (two-row)

⅔ lb. crystal malt

⅓ lb. wheat malt

¾ oz. Challenger (7% alpha acid) 60 minutes

⅔ oz. Challenger (7% alpha acid) 45 minutes

½ oz. Fuggles (5.50% alpha acid) 30 minutes

⅓ oz. Fuggles (5.50% alpha acid) 15 minutes

⅓ oz. Fuggles (5.50% alpha acid) ten minutes

⅓ oz. Fuggles (5.50% alpha acid) 0 minutes

½ tsp. Irish moss (Boil ten minutes)

1 oz. Fuggles (5.50% alpha acid) (Dry hop to secondary fermenter)

Nottingham Ale Yeast

¾ cup corn sugar (priming)

Directions:

1. Heat 4 gallons of water to 164 degrees.

2. Transfer heated water to mash lauter tun.

3. Mash crushed grains at 150 degrees for 60 minutes.

4. Recirculate, run off first wort (a little more than a gallon).

5. Heat 3 ¾ gallons of water to 168 degrees in a large pot. (This will be your sparge water.)

6. Collect first wort, and transfer it to your brew pot.

7. Gently add 168-degree sparge water to mash lauter tun.

8. Allow grains in mash lauter tun to rest for five minutes.

9. Recirculate wort in mash lauter tun.

10. Run off second wort, and gently add to brew pot. (You now have about 5 ¾ gallons of wort in the brew pot.)

11. Bring wort to a boil.

12. Add hops and Irish moss according to hop schedule to wort.

13. Boil for 90 minutes, following hop schedule as indicated in ingredient list.

14. Remove wort for heat after a total boil of 90 minutes.

15. Cool wort as quickly as possible to about 70 degrees.

16. Transfer wort to fermenter.

17. When wort reaches 70 degrees, aerate, and pitch yeast.

18. Ferment at 65 to 70 degrees for one week in primary fermenter.

19. Rack to secondary fermenter for one week.

20. Bottle condition with ¾ cup of corn sugar.

21. Allow two weeks to carbonate.

Conclusion

This book is just a starting point for those interested in establishing a home-brewing practice/hobby. The information here is intended to establish a basic knowledge of the craft of brewing and what is possible with just a few ingredients. This is only the tip of the huge iceberg that is home brewing.

You might start on this path and discover you only have the time and desire to engage in extract brewing. But many home brewers never go beyond this practice. With all of the ingredients and recipes for every conceivable  style of beer available to the home brewer, you can make excellent home-brewed beer using extracts and specialty grains.

For those of you who have a desire to take your brewing a little, partial mash brewing will offer more control over your final product while not requiring much in the way of additional equipment or ingredients. Although partial mash brewing might take a little more time than extract brewing, the practice is manageable for those that desire a little more control over the brewing process.

All-grain brewing is the pinnacle of the practice. It requires more time, space, equipment, and ingredient investment; the reward of having control over the entire process is what the all-grain brewer seeks.

Whether you brew strictly extract beer or you continue to go all out with the triple decoction mash technique, patience will be required. Beer is something that needs time. If you have ever enjoyed a six-month-old stout or a three-year-old lambic, you know that good things come to those who have the patience to wait.

Home brewing is a fun and rewarding practice. Though the instructions given in this book are specific, you will find that brewing is forgiving. Remember those individuals from Chapter 1 who brewed beer with nothing more than a few grains and a little rain? Do not be afraid to experiment and have fun. If you keep your equipment clean and sanitary, you will always come up with something worth tasting. With luck and patience, you also will brew something well worth sharing. Do not forget to share that brew. Your friends will be back for more. Drink up!

Resource Directory

Home-Brew Retailers

Alabama

Werner's Trading Company (**www.wernerstradingco.com**)
1115 4th St. S.W., Cullman, AL 35055
800-965-8796

The Wine Smith (**www.thewinesmith.biz**)
6800 A. Moffett Rd. US Highway 98, Mobile, AL 36618
251-645-5554

Arizona

Brewers Connection (**www.brewersconnection.com**)
1425 E. University Dr. #103, Tempe, AZ 85218
480-449-3720

4500 E. Speedway Blvd. #38, Tucson, AZ 85712
520-881-0255

Brew Your Own Brew and Wine (**http://brewyourownbrew.com**)
525 E. Baseline Rd. Suite 108, Gilbert, AZ 85233
480-497-0011

2564 N. Campbell Ave. Suite. 106, Tucson, AZ 85719
520-322-5049

Homebrewers Outpost & Mail Order Co. (**www.homebrewers.com**)
801 S. Milton Rd. Suite 2, Flagstaff, AZ 86001
928-213-0803

Hops & Tannins (**www.hopsandtannins.com**)
3434 W. Anthem Way. Suite 140, Anthem, AZ 85086
623-551-9857

Mile Hi Brewing Supplies (**http://milehibrewingsupplies.com**)
125 N. Cortez St., Prescott, AZ 86301
928-237-9029

What Ale's Ya (**www.whatalesya.com**)
6363 West Bell Rd., Suite 2, Glendale, AZ 85308
623-486-8016

Arkansas

Fermentables (**www.fermentables.com**)
3915 Crutcher St., North Little Rock, AR
501-758-6261

The Home Brewery (AR) (**www.thehomebrewery.com**)
455 E. Township Rd, Fayetteville, AR 72703
479-587-1440 or toll free 800-618-9474

California

Addison Homebrew Provisions (**http://homebrewprovisions.com**)
1328 E. Orangethorpe Ave., Fullerton, CA 92831
714-752-8446

The Beverage People (**www.thebeveragepeople.com**)
1851 Piner Rd. #D, Santa Rosa, CA 95403
707-544-2520 or toll free 800-544-1867

The Brewmeister (**www.folsombrewmeister.com**)
802A Reading St., Folsom, CA 95630
916-985-7299

1031 Junction Blvd, Suite 802
Roseville, CA 95678
916-780-7299

Culver City Home Brewing Supply (**www.brewsupply.com**)
4358 1/2 Sepulveda Blvd., Culver City, CA 90230
310-397-3453

4981 Eagle Rock Blvd
Los Angeles, CA 90041
323-258-2107

Doc's Cellar (**www.docscellar.com**)
855 Capitolio Way, San Luis Obispo, CA 93401
805-781-9974

Fermentation Solutions (**www.fermentationsolutions.com**)
2507 Winchester Blvd., Campbell, CA 95008
408-871-1400

The Good Brewer (**www.goodbrewer.com**)
2960 Pacific Ave., Livermore, CA 94550
925-373-0333

The Home Brew Shop (**www.chicohomebrewshop.com**)
1570 Nord Ave., Chico, CA 95926
530-342-3768

Hop Tech Homebrewing Supplies (**www.hoptech.com**)
6398 Dougherty Rd. Suite. 7, Dublin, CA 94568
925-875-0246 or toll free 800-DRY-HOPS (379-4677)

Hydrobrew (**www.hydrobrew.com**)
1319 S. Coast Highway, Oceanside, CA 92054
760-966-1885

MoreBeer! (Concord) (**http://morebeer.com**)
995 Detroit Ave., Unit G, Concord, CA 94518
925-671-4958

Murrieta Homebrew Emporium (**http://murrietahomebrew.com**)
38750 Sky Canyon Dr. Suite A, Murrieta, CA 92563
888-502-BEER (2337)

NorCal Brewing Solutions (**http://norcalbrewingsolutions.com**)
1768 Churn Creek Rd., Redding, CA 96002
530-243-BEER (2337)

Original Home Brew Outlet (**www.ehomebrew.com**)
5528 Auburn Blvd. #1, Sacramento, CA 95841
916-348-6322

O'Shea Brewing Company (**www.osheabrewing.com**)
28142 Camino Capistrano, Laguna Niguel, Ca 92677
949-364-4440

Seven Bridges Cooperative Certified Organic Brewing Ingredients
(**www.breworganic.com**)
325A River St., Santa Cruz, CA 95060
800-768-4409

Sierra Moonshine Homebrew Supplies (**www.sierramoonshine.com**)
12535 Loma Rica Dr., Grass Valley, CA 95945
530-274-9227

Stein Fillers (**www.steinfillers.com**)
4160 Norse Way, Long Beach, CA 90808
562-425-0588

Colorado

Beer at Home (**www.beerathome.com**)
1325 W. 121st Ave., Westminster, CO
720-872-9463

4393 S. Broadway, Englewood, CO
303-789-3676

Brew Hut (**www.thebrewhut.com**)
15120 E. Hampden Ave., Aurora, CO 80014
303-680-8898

Hops and Berries (**www.hopsandberries.com**)
125 Remington St., Fort Collins, CO
1833 E Harmony Rd, Unit 16, Fort Collins, CO
970-493-2484

Hop To It Homebrew (**www.stompthemgrapes.com**)
2900 Valmont Rd., Unit D2, Boulder, CO 80302
303-444-8888

Lil' Ole' Winemaker (**www.facebook.com/LilOleWinemaker**)
516 Main St., Grand Junction, CO
970-242-3754

Rocky Mountain Homebrew Supply
4631 S. Mason St. Suite B3, Fort Collins, CO
970-282-1191

Stomp Them Grapes (**www.stompthemgrapes.com**)
4731 Lipan St., Denver, CO 80211
303-433-6552

Connecticut

Beer & Wine Makers Warehouse (**www.bwmwct.com**)
290 Murphy Rd., Hartford, CT 06114
860-247-2969

Brew and Wine Hobby
12 Cedar Street, East Hartford, CT 06108
860-528-0592

Maltose Express (**www.maltose.com**)
246 Main St., Monroe, CT 06468
203-452-7332

Rob's Home Brew Supply (**www.robshomebrew.com**)
1 New London Rd. Unit #9, Salem, CT 06420
860-859-3990

Stomp N Crush (**www.stompncrush.com**)
140 Killingworth Turnpike (Rt 81), Clinton, CT 06413
860-552-4634

Delaware

How Do You Brew? (**www.howdoyoubrew.com**)
203 Louviers Dr., Newark, DE 19711
302-738-7009

Xtreme Brewing (**www.xtremebrewing.com**)
24612 Wiley Branch Rd., Millsboro, DE
302-934-8588

18501 Stamper Drive (Route 9), Lewes, Delaware
302-684-8936

Florida

AJ's Beer City Buzz (**www.ajsbeercitybuzz.com**)
221 Center St., Jupiter, FL 33458
561-575-2337

Beer and Winemaker's Pantry (**www.beerandwinemaking.com**)
9200 66th St. N., Pinellas Park, FL 33782
727-546-9117

BrewBox Miami (**www.brewboxmiami.com**)
8831 SW 129th St., Miami, FL
305-762-2859

BX Beer Depot (**www.bxbeerdepot.com**)
2964 2nd Ave. North, Lake Worth, FL 33461
561-965-9494

Just BREW It! (**www.justbrewitjax.com**)
2670-1 Rosselle St., Jacksonville, FL 32204
904-381-1983

1314 3rd St. N., Jacksonville Beach, FL 32250
904-435-4767

Southern Homebrew (**www.southernhomebrew.com**)
711 Canal Street, New Smyrna Beach, FL 32168
386-409-9100

Georgia

Barley & Vine (**www.barleynvine.com**)
1445 Rock Quarry Rd., Suite #201-203, Stockbridge, GA
770-507-5998

Beer & Wine Craft of Atlanta (**www.winecraftatl.com**)
5920 Roswell Rd. C-205, Atlanta, GA 30328
404-252-5606

Brew Depot — Home of Beer Necessities
(**www.beernecessities.com**)
10595 Old Alabama Rd. Connector, Alpharetta, GA 30022
770-645-1777 or toll free 877-450-2337

Brewmasters Warehouse (**www.brewmasterswarehouse.com**)
2145 Roswell Rd. Suite 320, Marietta, GA 30062
770-973-0072 or toll-free 877-973-0072

Just Brew It! (**http://aardvarkbrewing.com**)
1924 Highway 85, Suite 101, Jonesboro, GA 30238
770-719-0222 or toll free at 888-719-4645

Hawaii

Homebrew in Paradise (**www.homebrewinparadise.com**)
2646-B Kilihau St., Honolulu, HI
808-834-2739

Idaho

Brew Connoisseurs (**www.brewcon.com**)
3894 West State St., Boise, ID 83703
208-344-5141

Illinois

Bev Art Brewer & Winemaker Supply (**www.bev-art.com**)
10033 S. Western Ave. Chicago, IL 60643
773-233-7579

Chicagoland Winemakers Inc. (**www.chicagolandwinemakers.com**)
689 W. North Ave. Elmhurst, IL 60126
630-834-0507 or toll free 800-226-2739

Crystal Lake Health Food Store (**http://clhfs.com**)
25 E. Crystal Lake Ave., Crystal Lake, IL 60014
815-459-7942

Fox Valley Homebrew & Winery Supplies (**www.foxvalleybrew.com**)
14 W. Downer Pl. Suite 12, Aurora, IL 60505
630-892-0742

Home Brew Shop LTD (**www.homebrewshopltd.com**)
225 W. Main St., St. Charles, IL 60174
630-377-1338

Perfect Brewing Supply (**www.perfectbrewingsupply.com**)
619 E. Park Ave. Libertyville, IL 60048
847-816-7055

Somethings Brewn' (**www.somethingsbrewn.com**)
401 E. Main St., Galesburg, IL 61401
309-341-4118

Indiana

The Brewers Art Supply (**www.brewingart.com**)
1425 N. Wells St., Fort Wayne, IN 46808
260-426-7399

Butler Winery Inc. (**www.butlerwinery.com**)
6200 E. Robinson Rd., Bloomington, IN 47408
812-332-6660

Great Fermentations of Indiana (**www.greatfermentations.com**)
5127 E. 65th St., Indianapolis, IN 46220
317-257-WINE (9463)

Quality Wine and Ale Supply (**www.homebrewit.com**)
108 S. Elkhart Ave, Elkhart, IN 46516
574-295-9975

Superior Ag Co-op (**www.superiorag.com**)
5015 N. Saint Joseph Ave., Evansville, IN 47720
812-423-6481

Iowa

Beer Crazy (**www.gobeercrazy.com**)
3908 NW Urbandale Dr./100 St., Urbandale, IA 50322
515-331-0587

Bluff Street Brew Haus (**www.bluffbrewhaus.com**)
372 Bluff St., Dubuque, IA 52001
563-582-5420

Kansas

Bacchus & Barleycorn Ltd. (**www.bacchus-barleycorn.com**)
6633 Nieman Rd., Shawnee, KS 66203
913-962-2501

Homebrew Pro Shoppe (**www.brewcat.com**)
2061 E. Santa Fe St., Olathe, KS 66062
913-768-1090 or toll free 866-BYO-BREW

Kentucky

My Old Kentucky Homebrew
(**www.myoldkentuckyhomebrew.com**)
361 Baxter Ave., Louisville, KY
502-589-3434

Winemakers & Beermakers Supply (**www.winebeersupply.com**)
9475 Westport Rd., Louisville, KY 40241
502-425-1692

Louisiana

Brewstock (**www.brewstock.com**)
3800 Dryades St., New Orleans, LA 70118
504-208-2788

Maine

Maine Brewing Supply (**www.brewbrewbrew.com**)
542 Forest Ave., Portland, ME
207-791-2739

Natural Living Center
209 Longview Dr., Bangor, ME 04401
207-990-2646

Maryland

Annapolis Home Brew (**www.annapolishomebrew.com**)
836 Ritchie Highway Suite 19, Severna Park, MD 21146
410-975-0930 or toll free 800-279-7556

Flying Barrel (**www.flyingbarrel.com**)
1781 C North Market St., Frederick, MD 21701
301-663-4491

Maryland Homebrew (**http://stores.mdhb.com**)
6770 Oak Hall Lane, Columbia, MD 21045
410-290-3768 or toll free 888-BREW-NOW (273-9669)

Massachusetts

Beer and Wine Hobby (**www.beer-wine.com**)
155 T New Boston St., Woburn, MA 01801
781-933-8818 or toll free 800-523-5423

Beer & Winemaking Supplies Inc. (**www.beer-winemaking.com**)
154 King St., Northampton, MA 01060
413-586-0150 or toll free 800-473-BREW (2739)

Modern Homebrew Emporium (**www.beerbrew.com**)
2304 Massachusetts Ave., Cambridge, MA 02140
617-498-0400 or toll free 800-462-7397

NFG Home Brew Supplies (**www.nfghomebrew.com**)
72 Summer St., Leominster, MA 01453
978-840-1955 or toll free 866-559-1955

Strange Brew Beer & Winemaking Supplies (**www.home-brew.com**)
416 Boston Post Rd East/Route 20, Marlboro, MA 01752
888-BREWING (273-9464)

West Boylston Homebrew Emporium (**www.beerbrew.com**)
45 Sterling St. Suite 9, West Boylston, MA 01583
508-835-3374

The Witches Brew (**www.thewitchesbrew.com**)
12 Maple Ave., Foxboro, MA 02035
508-543-0433

Michigan

Adventures in Homebrewing (**www.homebrewing.org**)
23869 Van Born Rd. Taylor, MI 48180
6071 Jackson Rd., Ann Arbor, MI 48103
313-277-2739

Bell's General Store (**http://bellsbeer.com/store**)
355 E. Kalamazoo Ave., Kalamazoo, MI
269-382-5712

Brewer's Edge Homebrew Supply LLC
(**www.brewersedgehomebrew.com**)
650 Riley St. Suite E, Holland, MI 49424
616-805-8278

Brew Gadgets (**http://brewgadgets.com**)
328 S. Lincoln Ave., Lakeview, MI 48850
866-591-8247

Cap N Cork Homebrew Supply (**www.capncorkhomebrew.com**)
16812 21 Mile Rd., Macomb, MI 48044
586-286-5202

Hopman's Beer & Wine Making Supply
(**www.hopmanssupply.com**)
4690 W. Walton Blvd., Waterford, MI 48329
248-674-4677

Kuhnhenn Brewing Co. (**www.kbrewery.com**)
5919 Chicago Rd., Warren, MI 48092
586-979-8361

Michigan Brewing Co. (**www.michiganbrewing.com**)
402 Washington Square South, Lansing, MI 48933
517-977-1349

The Red Salamander (**www.theredsalamander.com**)
902 E. Saginaw Highway, Grand Ledge, MI 48837
517-627-2012

Siciliano's Market (**www.sicilianosmkt.com**)
2840 Lake Michigan Dr. NW, Grand Rapids, MI 49504
616-453-9674

Minnesota

Midwest Homebrewing Supplies (**www.midwestsupplies.com**)
5825 Excelsior Blvd. Minneapolis, MN 55416
888-449-2739

Northern Brewer Ltd. (**www.northernbrewer.com**)
6021 Lyndale Ave S, Minneapolis, MN 55419
651-223-6114 or toll free 800-681-2739

Still-H$_2$O Inc. (**http://still-h2o.com**)
14375 N. 60th St., Stillwater, MN 55082
651-351-2822

Missouri

Home Brewery (**www.homebrewery.com**)
1967 Boat St., Ozark, MO 65721
417-581-0963 or toll free 800-321-2739

Homebrew Supply of Southeast Missouri LLC
(**www.homebrewsupply.biz**)
3463 State Highway. FF, Jackson, MO 63755
573-579-9398

St. Louis Wine & Beermaking LLC
(**www.wineandbeermaking.com**)
231 Lamp and Lantern Village, Chesterfield, MO 63017
636-230-8277 or toll free 888-622-WINE (9463)

Nebraska

Fermenter's Supply & Equipment (**www.fermenterssupply.com**)
8410 K Plaza #10, Omaha, NE 68127
402-593-9171

Kirk's Brew (**www.kirksbrew.com**)
1150 Cornhusker Highway, Lincoln, NE 68521
402-476-7414

New Hampshire

Fermentation Station (**www.2ferment.net**)
72 Main St., Meredith, NH 03253
603-279-4028

Kettle to Keg (**www.kettletokeg.com**)
123 Main St., Pembroke, NH 03275
603-485-2054

Smoke N Barley (**www.smokenbarley.com**)
485 Laconia Rd., Tilton, NH
603-524-5004

Yeastern Homebrew Supply (**www.yeasternhomebrewsupply.com**)
4 Franklin Plaza, Dover, NH 03820
603-343-2956

New Jersey

The Brewer's Apprentice (**www.brewapp.com**)
865 Route 33 W. Suite 4, Freehold, NJ 07728
732-863-9411

Corrado's Home Beer and Winemaking Center
(**www.corradosmarket.com/home/store-wine.html**)
600 Getty Ave., Clifton, NJ 07011
973-340-0848

Rubino's Homemade Wine & Beer Supply
(**www.makewinebeer.com**)
2919 Route 206 Store #405, Columbus NJ 08022
609-261-8420

Tap It Homebrew Supply Shop (**www.tapithomebrew.com**)
144 Philadelphia Ave., Egg Harbor City, NJ 08215
609-593-3697

New Mexico

Santa Fe Homebrew Supply (**http://santafehomebrew.com**)
6820 Cerrillos Rd. Suite #4, Santa Fe, NM 87507
505-473-2268

Southwest Grape & Grain
(**http://www.southwestgrapeandgrain.com/**)
2801-N Eubank Blvd NE, Albuquerque, NM, NM 87112
505-332-BREW (2739)

Victor's Grape Arbor (**www.victorsgrapearbor.com**)
2436 San Mateo Pl. NE, Albuquerque, NM 87110
505-883-0000

New York

American Homesteader (**www.americanhomesteader.net**)
6767 State Highway 12, Norwich, NY 13815
607-334-9941

Doc's Homebrew Supplies (**www.docsbrew.com**)
451 Court St., Binghamton, NY 13904
607-722-2476

E.J. Wren Homebrewer Inc. (**www.ejwren.com**)
209 Oswego St., Liverpool, NY 13088
800-724-6875

Homebrew Emporium (**www.beerbrew.com**)
470 N. Greenbush Rd. Rensselaer, NY 12144
800-462-7397

Niagara Tradition Homebrewing Supplies (**http://nthomebrew.com**)
1296 Sheridan Dr., Tonawanda, NY 14217
716-877-8767 or toll free 800-283-4418

Pantano's Wine Grapes & Home Brew
(**http://www.pantanosbeerwine.com**)
249 Route 32 S, New Paltz, NY 12561
845-706-5152

Party Creations (**www.partycreations.net**)
345 Rokeby Rd., Red Hook, NY 12571
845-758-0661

Saratoga Zymurgist (**www.saratogaz.com**)
112 Excelsior Ave., Saratoga Springs, NY 12866
518-580-9785

North Carolina

Alternative Beverage (**http://ebrew.com**)
1500 River Dr., Belmont, NC 28012
704-527-2337 or toll free 800-365-2739

American Brewmaster Inc. (**www.americanbrewmaster.com**)
3021-5 Stony Brook Dr., Raleigh, NC 27604
919-850-0095

Asheville Brewers Supply (**www.ashevillebrewers.com**)
712-B Merrimon Ave., Asheville, NC 28804
828-285-0515

Beer & Wine Hobbies, Int'l
(**www.ebrew.com/retail/beer_wine_hobbies.htm**)
4450 S. Blvd. Charlotte, NC 28209
168-S Norman Station Blvd., Mooresville, NC 28117
704-527-2337

Bull City Homebrew (**www.bullcityhomebrew.com**)
1906 NC Highway. 54 Suite 200-B, Durham, NC 27713
919-682-0300

Hops & Vines (**www.hopsandvines.net**)
797 Haywood Rd. Suite 100, West Asheville, NC 28806
828-252-5275

Ohio

Abruzzo's Wine & Home Brew Supply (**http://abruzzos.com**)
137 East Ave., Tallmadge, OH 44278
330-678-6400

Grape and Granary (**www.grapeandgranary.com**)
915 Home Ave., Akron, OH 44310
800-695-9870

The Hops Shack (**www.hopsshack.com**)
1687 Marion Rd., Bucyrus, OH 44820
419-617-7770

Main Squeeze (**http://mainsqueezeonline.com**)
229 Xenia Ave., Yellow Springs, OH
937-767-1607

Listermann Manufacturing Co. (**www.listermann.com**)
1621 Dana Ave., Cincinnati, OH 45212
513-731-1130

Miami Valley BrewTensils (**www.brewtensils.com**)
2617 S. Smithville Rd., Dayton, OH 45420
937-252-4724

Paradise Brewing Supplies (**www.paradisebrewingsupplies.com**)
7766 Beechmont Ave., Cincinnati, OH 45255
513-232-7271

The Pumphouse
336 Elm St., Struthers, OH 44471
330-755-3642 or toll free 800-947-8677

Shrivers Beer & Wine Supplies (McConnelsville)
(**http://shriversbeerwinesupply.com**)
105 N. Kennebec Ave., McConnelsville, OH 43756
740-962-2552 or toll free 800-845-0556

42 Watkins St., Nelsonville, OH 45764
740-753-2484

510 N. Main St., New Lexington, OH 43764
740-342-5133 or toll free 800-845-0561

406 Brighton Blvd., Zanesville, OH 43701
740-452-3691 or toll-free 800-845-0560

Titgemeier's Inc. (**www.titgemeiers.com**)
701 Western Ave., Toledo, OH
419-243-3731

Oklahoma

High Gravity Homebrewing and Winemaking Supplies
(**www.highgravitybrew.com**)
7164 S. Memorial Dr. Tulsa, OK
918-461-2605

Learn to Brew LLC (**www.learntobrew.com**)
2307 S. I-35 Frontage Rd., Moore, OK 73160
405-793-2337

Oregon

Above the Rest Homebrewing Supplies
(**http://abovetheresthomebrewing.net**)

11945 SW Pacific Highway #235, Tigard, OR 97223
503-968-2736

Brew Brothers Homebrew Products LLC
(**http://brewbrothers.biz**)
2020 NW Aloclek Dr. Suite 104, Hillsboro, OR 97124
971-222-3434 or toll free 888-528-8443

Corvallis Brewing Supply (**www.lickspigot.com**)
119 SW 4th Street Corvallis, OR 97333
541-758-1674

F.H. Steinbart Co. (**http://fhsteinbart.com**)
234 SE 12th Ave., Portland, OR 97214
503-232-8793

Grains Beans & Things (**www.grains-n-beans.com**)
820 Crater Lake Ave. Suite 113, Medford, OR 97504
541-499-6777

Main Street Homebrew Supply Co. (**www.mainbrew.com**)
23596 NW Clara Ln., Hillsboro, OR 97124
503-648-4254

Valley Vintner & Brewer (**www.brewabeer.com**)
30 E. 13th Ave., Eugene, OR 97401
541-484-3322

Pennsylvania

Bald Eagle Brewing Co. (**www.baldeaglebrewingco.com**)
315 Chestnut St., Mifflinburg, PA 17844
570-966-3156

Beer Solutions Inc (**www.beersolutionsinc.com**)
507 Blackman St., Wilkes-Barre, PA 18701
570-825-5509

Country Wines (**www.countrywines.com**)
3333 Babcock Blvd., Pittsburgh, PA 15237
866-880-7404

Homebrew4Less.com LLC (**www.homebrew4less.com**)
890 Lincoln Way West, Chambersburg, PA 17202
717-504-8534

Keystone Homebrew Supply (Bethlehem)
(**www.keystonehomebrew.com**)
599 Main St., Bethlehem, PA 18018
610-997-0911

435 Doylestown Rd., Montgomeryville, PA 18936
215-855-0100

Lancaster Homebrew (**http://lancasterhomebrew.com**)
1944 Lincoln Highway E., Lancaster, PA
717-517-8785

Mr. Steve's Homebrew & Wine Supplies (Lancaster)
(**www.mrsteves.com**)
2104 Spring Valley Rd., Lancaster PA 17601
717-397-4818
2944 Whiteford Rd., Suite 5, York, PA 17402
717-751-2255

Porter House Brew Shop (**www.porterhousebrewshop.com**)
1284 Perry Highway, Portersville, PA 16051
724-368-9771

Ruffled Wine & Brewing Supplies (**www.ruffledhomebrewing.com**)
616 Allegheny River Blvd., Oakmont, PA 15139
412-828-7412

Scotzin Bros. (**www.scotzinbros.com**)
65 C N. Fifth St., Lemoyne, PA 17043
717-737-0483 or toll free 800-791-1464

South Hills Brewing Supply (Greentree)
(**www.southhillsbrewing.com**)
2212 Noblestown Rd., Pittsburgh, PA 15205
412-937-0773

2526 Mosside Blvd. Pittsburgh, PA 15146
412-374-1240

Universal Carbonic Gas Co.
614 Gregg Ave., Reading, PA
610-372-2565

Weak Knee Home Brewing Supplies Inc.
(**http://weakkneehomebrew.com**)
1300 N. Charlotte St., Pottstown, PA 19464
610-327-1450

Windy Hill Wine Making (**http://windyhillwine.net**)
10998 Perry Highway, Meadville, PA 16335
814-337-6871

Wine and Beer Emporium (**www.winebeeremporium.com**)
100 Ridge Rd. #27, Chadds Ford, PA 19317
610-558-BEER (2337)

Wine and Beer Makers Outlet
(**www.wineandbeermakersoutlet.com**)
202 S. 3rd St., Coopersburg, PA 18036
484-863-1070

Wine, Barley & Hops Homebrew Supply
(**www.winebarleyandhops.com**)
248 Bustleton Pike, Feasterville, PA 19053
215-322-4780

Rhode Island

Adamsville Wine and Spirits
81 Stone Church Rd., Little Compton, RI
401-635-2109

Blackstone Valley Brewing Supplies
(**www.blackstonevalleybrewing.com**)
403 Park Ave., Woonsocket, RI 02895
401-765-3830

South Carolina

Bet-Mar Liquid Hobby Shop (**www.liquidhobby.com**)
736-F St. Andrews Rd., Columbia, SC
803-798-2033

South Dakota

GoodSpirits Fine Wine & Liquor (**http://gsfw.com**)
3300 S. Minnesota Ave., Sioux Falls, SD 57105
605-339-1500

Tennessee

All Seasons Gardening & Brewing Supply
(**www.allseasonsnashville.com**)
924 8th Ave. S., Nashville, TN
615-214-5465 or toll free 800-790-2188

Texas

Austin Homebrew Supply (**www.austinhomebrew.com**)
9129 Metric Blvd., Austin, TX 78758
512-300-BREW (2739) or toll free 800-890-BREW (2739)

DeFalco's Home Wine and Beer Supplies (**www.defalcos.com**)
8715 Stella Link, Houston, TX
713-668-9440

Fine Vine Wines — The Winemaker's Toy Store
(**www.finevinewines.com**)
1300 N. Interstate 35-E Suite 106, Carrollton, TX 75006
866-417-1114

Homebrew Headquarters (**www.homebrewhq.com**)
300 N. Coit Rd. Suite 134, Richardson, TX 75080
972-234-4411

Home Brew Party (**www.homebrewparty.com**)
15150 Nacogdoches Rd. Suite 130, San Antonio, TX 78247
210-650-9070

Keg Cowboy (**www.kegcowboy.com**)
2017 1/2 S. Shepherd, Houston, TX
281-888-0507

Utah

The Beer Nut Inc. (**www.beernut.com**)
1200 S. State Salt Lake City, UT 84111
801-531-8182

Virginia

Blue Ridge Hydroponics & Home Brewing Co.
(**www.blueridgehydroponics.com**)
5327 D Williamson Rd., Roanoke, VA 24012
540-265-2483

HomeBrewUSA (**www.homebrewusa.com**)
96 W. Mercury Blvd., Hampton, VA 23669
757-788-8001

5802 E. Virginia Beach Blvd. #115, Norfolk, VA 23502
757-459-2739

Fermentation Trap Inc. (**www.fermentationtrap.com**)
6420 Seminole Trail #12, Barboursville, VA
434-985-2192 or toll free 888-985-2192

Jay's Brewing Supplies (**www.jaysbrewing.com**)
9790 Center St., Manassas, VA 20124
703-543-2663

myLHBS (myLocalHomeBrewShop) (**www.mylhbs.com**)
6201 Leesburg Pike #3, Falls Church, VA
703-241-3874

WeekEnd Brewer — Your 'At Home' Beer & Wine Supply
(**www.weekendbrewer.com**)
4205 West Hundred Rd., Chester, VA 23831
804-796-9760 or toll free 800-320-1456

Wild Wolf Brewing Company (**www.wildwolfbeer.com**)
2773A Rockfish Valley Highway, Nellysford, VA
434-361-0088

Washington

Bader Beer & Wine Supply Inc. (**http://baderbrewing.com**)
711 Grand Blvd, Vancouver, WA 98661
360-750-1551 or toll free 800-596-3610

The Beer Essentials (**www.thebeeressentials.com**)
2624 112th St. #E-1, Lakewood, WA 98499
253-581-4288 or toll free 800-685-BREW (2739)

Homebrew Heaven (**www.homebrewheaven.com**)
9109 Evergreen Way, Everett, WA 98204
425-355-8865

Larry's Brewing Supply (**www.larrysbrewsupply.com**)
7405 S. 212th St. #103, Kent, WA 98032
253-872-6846 or toll free 800-441-BREW (2739)

Mountain Homebrew & Wine Supply
(**http://mountainhomebrew.com**)
8530 122nd Ave., NE B2, Kirkland, WA 98033
877-DO-U-BREW (368-2739)

Northwest Brewers Supply (**www.nwbrewers.com**)
1006 6th St., Anacortes, WA 98221
360-293-0424 or toll free 800-460-7095

Yakima Valley Winery Supply
401 7th St., Prosser, WA 99350
509-786-2033

Wisconsin

House of Homebrew (**www.houseofhomebrew.com**)
410 Dousman St., Green Bay, WI 54303
920-435-1007

O'so Brewing Co. (**www.osobrewing.com**)
3028 Village Park Dr., Plover, WI 54467
715-254-2163

Northern Brewer Ltd. (Milwaukee) (**www.northernbrewer.com**)
1306 S. 108th St., Milwaukee, WI 53214
414-935-4099

The Purple Foot (**www.purplefootusa.com**)
3167 S. 92nd St., Milwaukee, WI 53227
414-327-2130

WindRiver Brewing Co. Inc. (**www.windriverbrew.com**)
861 10th Ave., Barron, WI 54812
800-266-4677

Wine & Hop Shop (**http://wineandhop.com**)
1931 Monroe St., Madison, WI 53711
608-257-0099 or toll free 800-657-5199

Web Equipment and ingredient Resources

The resources listed here are only a handful of the many equipment and ingredient resources available to the home-brew enthusiast. The best place to begin your search is at your local home-brew retailer. See the list above for a retailer in your area.

Brew Gadgets — **http://brewgadgets.com**

Homebrew Heaven — **http://store.homebrewheaven.com/beer-brewing-c56.aspx**

HomeBrewing.com — **www.homebrewing.com**

Kirk's Brew — **www.kirksbrew.com**

Midwest Homebrewing and Winemaking Supplies — **www.midwestsupplies.com**

More Beer! — **http://morebeer.com**

Northern Brewer — **www.northernbrewer.com**

Web Home-Brew Resources and Forums

Brew Your Own: The How-To Homebrew Beer Magazine. **www.byo.com**

BeerAdvocate: A global, grassroots network, powered by an independent community of beer enthusiasts and industry professionals who are dedicated to supporting and promoting beer. **http://beeradvocate.com**

Beer Utopia: The never-ending search for the best beer. **http://beerutopia.com**

BrewHeads: This website offers free calculators for such things as water volume and temperature, gravity, and alcohol content. **www.brewheads.com**

Brewprint: A tool for creating, organizing, and sharing beer brewing recipes. **www.brewprint.com/home**

HomeBrewTalk: A home-brewing beer and wine making civilized discussion community. **www.homebrewtalk.com**

Hopville: Hopville is home to beer recipes and the brewers who make them. **http://hopville.com**

John Palmer's *How to Brew*: An indispensable guide to home brewing. **www.howtobrew.com/intro.html**

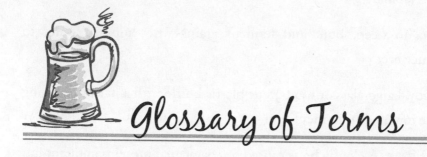

Glossary of Terms

adjunct. Ingredients added to a base beer recipe to help in flavoring and fermentation or to achieve a specific function, though not essential.

aerate. To add oxygen, usually by stirring.

airlock. Device that allows gas to escape from a fermenting vessel but stops any outside air from entering the vessel.

ale. Top-fermenting beer.

alpha acid. Chemical compound found in hops that give them their bitterness.

amylase. A digestive enzyme that aids in the conversion of starch into sugars.

attenuation. The measure of how much sugar is converted into alcohol by yeast in wort.

barley. A grain that is the primary ingredient in the brewing of beer.

beer. Alcoholic drink made with malted barley, water, yeast, and hops.

beta-acid. Chemical compound found in hops that contribute to a brew's aroma.

brew. To steep, boil, and ferment grains with hops in water to produce beer.

carboy. Large glass or food-grade plastic bottle with a narrow opening at the top used to ferment beer.

chill haze. A cloudy brew caused by coagulated proteins and tannins.

conditioning. Final stage of the brewing process when carbonation occurs.

decoction. The process of extracting by boiling.

diacetyl. A chemical byproduct of yeast fermentation.

diastatic (diastase). Enzymes in malt that convert starch to fermentable sugars.

dunkel. German for "dark."

dry hops. Hops added after the wort boil to add aroma to beer.

fermentatio. The conversion of sugar into alcohol and carbon dioxide by yeast.

final gravity. The density of beer in relation to the density of water after fermentation is complete.

flocculation. The tendency of yeast to clump together (flocculate) to form sediment at the bottom of the fermenter at the end of the fermentation cycle.

grist. Crushed grain used for mashing.

helles. German for "light."

hydrometer. Instrument used to measure the specific gravity of liquids,

international bitterness units (IBU). The measurement of the bitterness of beer. Technically, the measurement is 1 milligram of isomerized alpha acid in 1 liter of wort or brewed beer.

keg. A barrel, usually metal, meant to hold and dispense beer.

krausen. Foam that forms on top of fermenting beer.

krausening. The priming of beer with krausen at bottling time.

lager. From the German word for "to store," a style of beer fermented by bottom-fermenting yeast and brewed at cool or cold temperatures.

lagering. The fermentation, conditioning, and aging time of lager-style beer.

lauter. To separate the wort from the grain of mashing.

lauter tun. The vessel used to separate the wort from the grain after it is mashed.

liquor. The home-brewer's word for the water used to brew beer.

Lovibond. The scale used to measure the color of a beer — example. 60°L.

malt. Grain that has been germinated and dried for brewing and other uses.

mash(ing). The combination of grains and hot water used to convert starch to fermentable sugar in the brewing process.

modification. The alterations in cereal grain caused by germination during the process of malting.

original gravity. The density of beer in relation to the density of water before fermentation.

pitching. The term used to describe the addition of yeast to wort for fermentation.

primary fermentation. The first stage of the fermentation process.

priming. The act of adding sugar to fermented beer to help with carbonation.

racking. Transferring beer or wort to a fermenter or to bottles.

saccharification. The stage in the brewing process when complex carbohydrates are broken down into simple sugars.

sparge. To rinse wort grist in order to collect sugars from a mash.

starter. A mixture of wort and yeast used to spur fermentation.

step-mash. A procedure that involves sequences of temperature modification in order to achieve specific results from a mash.

tannin. Naturally occurring plant compounds that can cause bitterness and cloudiness in beer.

wort. Unfermented beer.

yeast. Single-celled fungi that convert sugars to CO_2 and alcohol.

Bibliography

Beechum, Drew. *The Everything Homebrewing Book*. Avon, Massachusetts: Adams Media, 2009.

Daniels, Ray. *Designing Great Beers*. Boulder, Colorado: Brewers Publications, 2000.

Lutzen, Karl F. and Mark Stevens. *Homebrew Favorites*. North Adams, Massachusetts: Storey Publishing, 1994.

Miller, Dave. *Homebrewing Guide*. North Adams, Massachusetts: Storey Publishing, 1995.

Moore, William. *Home Beermaking*. San Leandro, California: Ferment Press, 1991.

Palmer, John J. *How to Brew*. Boulder, Colorado: Brewers Publications, 2006.

Papazian, Charlie. *The Complete Joy of Homebrewing*. New York: HarperCollins Publishers, 2003.

Snyder, Stephen. *The Brewmaster's Bible*. New York: HarperCollins Publishers, 1997.

Author Biography

Richard Helweg has more than 25 years experience working in the nonprofit sector as an artistic director, managing director, and executive director. He is an award-winning playwright and has recently written… *And Justice for All, A History of the Supreme Court*, a book for young readers; and *How to Get Your Share of the $30-Plus Billion Being Offered by U.S. Foundations*. Richard lives in Lincoln, Nebraska, with his wife, Karen, and sons Aedan and Rory.

Index

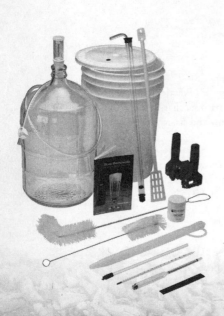